Lecture Notes of the Institute for Computer Sciences, Social Informatics and Telecommunications Engineering   64

Radu Popescu-Zeletin Idris A. Rai
Karl Jonas Adolfo Villafiorita (Eds.)

E-Infrastructures
and E-Services
for Developing Countries

Second International ICST Conference
AFRICOMM 2010
Cape Town, South Africa, November 25-26, 2010
Revised Selected Papers

 Springer

Volume Editors

Radu Popescu-Zeletin
Fraunhofer FOKUS, 10589 Berlin, Germany
E-mail: radu.popescu-zeletin@fokus.fraunhofer.de

Idris A. Rai
Makerere University, Kampala, Uganda
E-mail: rai@cit.mak.ac.ug

Karl Jonas
Fraunhofer FOKUS, Schloss Birlinghoven
53757 Sankt Augustin, Germany
E-mail: karl.jonas@fokus.fraunhofer.de

Adolfo Villafiorita
FBK Center for Information Technology
38100 Trento, Italy
E-mail: adolfo.villafiorita@fbk.eu

ISSN 1867-8211   e-ISSN 1867-822X
ISBN 978-3-642-23827-7   e-ISBN 978-3-642-23828-4
DOI 10.1007/978-3-642-23828-4

Springer Heidelberg Dordrecht London New York

Library of Congress Control Number: 2011935557

CR Subject Classification (1998): K.4, C.2, K.3, K.6, K.5, J.1

Typesetting: Camera-ready by author, data conversion by Scientific Publishing Services, Chennai, India

Printed on acid-free paper

Springer is part of Springer Science+Business Media (www.springer.com)

Preface

Africa is considered the remaining land of opportunities that provides a very large untouched market for e-infrastructure and e-services solutions. We have recently witnessed a wave of submarine cable initiatives to bring high-speed Internet access in the continent. Due to its geography as well as the popularity of mobile telephony in the continent, however, Africa is bound to remain a wireless continent and is therefore one of the most important markets for emerging high-speed wireless and mobile communication technologies. In this scenario, new, affordable, and innovative mobile services are increasingly needed to close the gap in the digital divide currently engulfing the continent.

Communities in Africa experience unique socio-economic challenges compared to communities in other continents, developed and developing alike. Therefore, ICT needs to be exploited differently and customized to address these challenges. Technologies of high contemporary relevance include those that enable affordable mobile broadband access and that provide enriched mobile handsets with services such as mobile banking, mobile health, mobile learning, etc.

For largely economical reasons, Africa needs highly adaptive, self-configuring, energy-efficient, and scalable technologies that require minimal manual operation and maintenance. Wireless mesh networking, mobile ad-hoc networking, or mobile peer-to-peer networking therefore some of the key areas that can lead to numerous relevant services in the future. Cloud computing and its services are emerging and highly promising technologies for economically constrained communities like those in Africa. More research work is required in that area.

In addition, there is a need for effective policies and regulations within African countries to enable not only widely accessible e-infrastructures and e-services to the poor and to remote communities, but also to protect from their misuse through enforcement of relevant security measures as well.

Researchers and practitioners across the world, therefore, live in a very critical moment with regard to the continent. Africa is, more than ever, in need of cutting-edge and relevant e-infrastructures, e-services, and enabling policies. AFRICOMM is a series of annual conferences established in 2009 to provide a platform that will actively contribute to such needs through dissemination of quality research findings. Its contributions have been published in Springer's *Lecture Notes on ICST*.

This book contains the proceedings of AFRICOMM 2010, which was held in Cape Town. The book contains high-quality papers thanks to the effective and highly specialized technical Program Committee which also diligently selected the best paper that was awarded at AFRICOMM 2010. The best paper is entitled "Connecting Mobile Phones via Carrier-Grade Meshed Wireless Back-Haul Networks," by Mathias Kretschmer, Christian Niephaus, Karl Jonas, and Thorsten Horstmann from Fraunhofer FOKUS, Sankt Augustin, Germany

May 2011   Radu Popescu-Zeletin
                                                                  Idris A. Rai
                                                                  Karl Jonas
                                                             Adolfo Villafiorita

Organization

Steering Committee

Imrich Chlamtac	CREATE-NET, Italy
Salomao Julio Manhica	UTICT, Mozambique
Fausto Giunchiglia	University of Trento, Italy
Paolo Traverso	FBK, Italy
Alessandro Zorer	CREATE-NET, Italy

Organizing Committee

Conference General Chair

Radu Popescu-Zeletin	Fraunhofer FOKUS, Germany

TPC Chair

Idris A. Rai	Makerere University, Uganda

TPC Track Chairs

Adolfo Villafiorita	FBK Center for Information Technology, Italy
Karl Jonas	Fraunhofer FOKUS, Germany

Sponsorship Chair

Alessandro Zorer	CREATE-NET, Italy

Local Chair

Darelle van Greunen	N. Mandela Metropolitan University, South Africa

Workshops and Demos Chair

Dirk Elias	Fraunhofer, Portugal

Posters and Panels Chair

Hans Schotten	University of Kaiserslautern, Germany

Technical Program Committee

Timo Ojala	University of Oulu, Finland
Omar Fakih Hamad	University of Dar-es-Salaam, Tanzania
Ntsibane Ntlatlapa	Meraka Institute, South Africa
Emmanuel Tonye	Yaounde 1 University, Cameroon
Thomas Magedanz	Fraunhofer FOKUS, Germany
Guy Tanonkou	ACSAL, Luxembourg
Evika Karamagioli	Gov2u, Greece
Komminist Weldemariam	FBK Center for Information, Technology, Italy
Lasse Berntzen	Vestfold University College, Norway
Robert Krimmer	E-Voting.CC, Austria
Joseph Migga Kizza	The University of Tennessee at Chattanooga, USA
Michael Best	Georgia Tech, USA
Rehema Baguma	Makerere University, Uganda
Love Ekenberg	Stockholm University, Sweden
Lasse Berntzen	Vestfold University College, Norway

Table of Contents

ICT Business Models and Open-Access

Connecting Mobile Phones via Carrier-Grade Meshed Wireless Back-Haul Networks

Mathias Kretschmer, Peter Hasse, Christian Niephaus,
Thorsten Horstmann, and Karl Jonas

Fraunhofer FOKUS, Sankt Augustin, Germany
{mathias.kretschmer,peter.hasse,christian.niephaus,
thorsten.horstmann,karl.jonas}@fokus.fraunhofer.de

Abstract. Meshed wireless back-haul networks are seen as an affordable technology to bring Internet connectivity into rural and previously
unconnected regions. To date, the main focus is to provide access to classical services such as the WWW or email. Access to such services requires
the users to use a personal computer or a recent smart phone. Especially
in developing regions, the prevailing end user device is a mobile phone.
In order to connect mobile phones to an IP-based back-haul network, the
network access points must provide a mobile phone air interface which
is usually based on GSM or UMTS. In order to avoid dependence on a
costly 3GPP infrastructure, we propose to deploy GSM or 3GPP nano
cells in order to terminate the mobile phone protocols immediately at
the mesh access points. Hence, the voice or data traffic can be carried
over IP-based networks using open protocols such as SIP and RTP. In
this paper we present a meshed wireless back-haul network with access
points that have been equipped with GSM nano-cells. The voice traffic
generated by the mobile phones is carried across the mesh in parallel to
typical web or video traffic. In this paper we evaluate the QoS handling
received by the voice calls across our multi-hop wireless testbed and show
that our architecture can provide the resource isolation required to offer
uninterrupted VoIP services in parallel to typical Internet traffic.

1 Motivation

Wireless Mesh Networks (WMNs) have matured considerably and their visi-
bility attracts researchers as well as commercial service providers. Resilience,
self-configuration and maintenance combined with potentially lower equipment
as well as operational costs are seen as major advantages compared to traditional
commercially operated wireless networks. Especially in emerging or so far unconnected regions, WMNs have the potential to serve as a cost-efficient solution
to bridge the digital divide. The lack of access to the worldwide communication
infrastructure in emerging countries is a limiting factor for their improvement
in education, health and economics.

The majority of potential customers in developing regions owns a mobile
phone, but no personal computer. Therefore it is crucial to enable regular mobile

R. Popescu-Zeletin et al. (Eds.): AFRICOMM 2010, LNICST 64, pp. 1–10, 2011.

phones to directly connect to the network, without the need of any additional software or modification on the mobile phone. However, in Africa for example the geographical conditions make a typical GSM deployment like it has been done in Europe or North America very expensive, since especially in rural areas the distances between villages are rather large, typically in the scale of several hundred kilometers. Thus, a regular GSM cell would cover only a comparable small number of customers which makes it unprofitable for most common operators. We therefore propose a new network architecture that incorporates nano-Base Transceiver Station (BTS) cells which are connected with each other and to the Internet via a Wireless Back-Haul (WiBack) network.

2   Architecture

WiBack builds upon the architecture defined by the EU FP7 project CARrier grade wireless MEsh Network (CARMEN)[3] which is based on an extended version of the IEEE 802.21 standard on the control plane and a light-weight implementation of Multi Protocol Label Switching (MPLS) [11][10] on the data plane. The access point nodes have been fitted with GSM air interfaces terminating the mobile phone protocols right at the access point so that the VoIP traffic can be forwarded via the mesh using open protocols such as Session Initiation Protocol (SIP)[12] in combination with Real-time Transport Protocol (RTP)[13] or alternatively Inter-Asterisk eXchange Version 2 (IAX2)[9]. In the following sections we will summarize the WiBack architecture and then describe the integration with the GSM air interface.

2.1   Carrier-Grade Wireless Back-Haul Mesh Network

The WiBack architecture builds on proven standards which have been extended to support heterogeneous wireless technologies. The core of the control plane adopts and extends IEEE 802.21, which allows for a hardware-independent and modular cross-layer architecture design, see Figure 1. The network management components such as the Topology Management Function (TMF), Routing, Monitoring and Mobility Management can be implemented as modules on top of an abstraction layer using the IEEE 802.21 messaging mechanism. This differentiates our approach from typical Network Layer routing protocols, which integrate similar functionality in one protocol and are often agnostic to physical hardware capabilities.

2.2   IEEE 802.21

One of the main goals of IEEE 802.21 is to provide link layer intelligence and abstraction for the upper layers. This should allow for a more intelligent decision making capability leading to more reliable and efficient hand-overs between heterogeneous access networks. However, the concepts and architecture of IEEE 802.21 can also be exploited for other purposes besides hand-overs such as

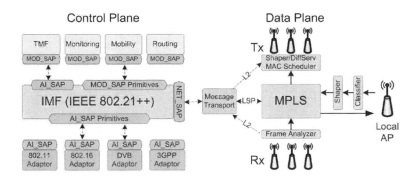

Fig. 1. IMF extends the IEEE 802.21 MIHF by Module-to-Module Communication

the management of heterogeneous networks including security, emergency services and power management relying on the resilient messaging characteristics specified in the IEEE 802.21 standard. Each of those topics have been studied within sub-groups of the IEEE 802.21 working group with the target of preparing amendments to the standard.

The IEEE 802.21 messaging service as well as the majority of the defined primitives can also be utilized for non-hand-over related purposes, such as managing local and remote radio technologies in a media independent manner. Therefore, WiBack builds on the general IEEE 802.21 architecture introducing new primitives or messaging service extensions where needed.

As depicted in Figure 1, the WiBack Interface Management Function (IMF) extends the IEEE 802.21 Media Independent Handover Function (MIHF) with primitives specific to wireless network management, therefore the name IMF has been chosen to reflect its responsibilities which go beyond *Media Independent Hand-overs*. This amendment to IEEE 802.21 provides a single interface for realizing Mobile Terminal (MT) hand-overs as well as building and managing a heterogeneous wireless networks.

2.3 Network Resource Management

Traffic Engineering (TE)[2] deals with network engineering and performance evaluation. It's objective is to facilitate reliable network operation. WiBack is designed upon traffic engineering principals which have been adapted to the requirements of volatile wireless links.

The resource utilization can be configured according to operator policies. The standard configuration builds on the over-provisioning paradigm to avoid queueing and loss inside the mesh network. Hence, at the ingress nodes, traffic is classified and shaped to fit into the envelope of admitted resources. The forwarding function at each intermediate mesh node performs prioritized DiffServ-like queueing as well as proper shaping to smooth out transient states of congestions due to traffic bursts, etc.

Constraint based routing computes paths through a network topology fulfilling a set of constraints. Instead of simple hop count metrics those constraints maybe be expressed as minimum bandwidth, maximum delay, or similar. To optimize the network resource utilization, the Path Computation Element (PCE)[4] architecture uses centralized routing entities.

Unlike hierarchical prefix routing which is typically associated with Internet Protocol (IP) packet routing in the Internet, MPLS tags packets with a 32 bit wide label based on which forwarding is then performed in intermediate routers. MPLS operates at an Open Systems Interconnection (OSI) layer which is often referred to as Layer 2.5, between the data link and the network layer and MPLS labels are positioned between link layer headers and the headers of the encapsulated packet. The name MPLS refers to its independence from both layer 2 and layer 3 protocols, which makes MPLS an interesting candidate for data forwarding in a heterogeneous wireless back-haul network while enforcing Quality of Service (QoS) and paths computed by a centralized network management component. Label-Switched Paths (LSPs) are usually set up and managed using RSVP-TE[1].

The above mentioned protocols are mainly targeted for wired or wireless operator networks where link properties are usually constant and the changing traffic patterns are the main source of dynamic network state changes. acWiBack needs to address an additional source of potentially frequent state changes introduced by the more volatile nature of wireless technologies such as IEEE 802.11. WiBack utilizes a wireless cell resource model to account for link quality fluctuations as well as the MAC layer overhead introduced by shared-medium technologies. When computing new LSPs this model is deployed by the centralized path computation components mostly located at the gateways nodes, which are providing the connection to the operator's core network. For example, typical Voice-over-IP (VoIP) flows with their rather small packets will block larger amounts of cell resources on typical Enhanced Distributed Coordination Access (EDCA) WLAN links due to the overhead of the contention based MAC layer.

As shown in [7], receiver-side wireless link monitoring is a crucial component to monitor WiBack links. For each link triggers are installed at the receiving node which inform the gateway node if the performance drops below a certain threshold so that the link can no longer carry the admitted QoS traffic. In such a case the affected LSPs will be re-routed onto backup paths.

While operator networks require engineers for planning and initial configuration, WiBack utilizes self-management functionality such as self-description, self-configuration and self-healing to minimize the need for technicians. This functionality is provided by the TMF which is implemented at each mesh node. The main TMF process is executed at the centralized gateway node detects and joins mesh nodes in a ring-based approach where direct neighbors are joined first, followed by two-hop neighbors, then three-hop neighbors and so forth. Upon detection and registration of a new mesh node its radio interfaces are configured to match the TMF's optimization criterion, i.e. highest throughput or highest robustness. Once the radio interfaces of the new node have been configured and links have been established with neighboring mesh nodes those links are being made available to the path computation module which may allocate resource and place LSPs onto them.

2.4 GSM Nano-Cells and OpenBTS

A typical GSM setup requires a hierarchy of components that have to be available in order to operate and manage the network, e.g. Home Location Register (HLR) or Mobile-services Switching Centre (MSC). For the designated deployment scenario this has two major drawbacks: First, the required Hard- and Software is very cost-extensive which makes a deployment of a regular GSM network unappealing for operators due to the expected small number of customers per cell. Second, all components of the typical GSM architecture have to be available at all time. Thus, a failure of a single component can lead to a complete network failure. Particularly if nodes have no constant power supply but are only equipped with a solar cell leading to a higher failure rate this becomes much more important. We therefore propose in our approach to carry the voice traffic over a WiBack network as described in section 2 and to terminate the GSM based communication right in the access point and use SIP or IAX2 to carry the voice data to its destination or a connection point to the Public Switched Telephone Network (PSTN).

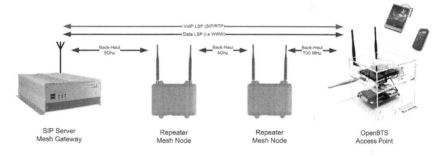

Fig. 2. Integration of an OpenBTS-based GSM cell into a WiBack Access Point

Our actual setup as depicted in Figure 2 makes use of the OpenBTS[1] project software in combination with the Universal Software Radio Peripheral (USRP)[2]. This gives us the advantage of a GSM to SIP adaption directly at the access point without the need of any further GSM-related software components anywhere else in the architecture. The voice traffic is converted in the AP and transported via a dedicated VoIP LSP to its destination.

Due to lower costs and the flexibility of WiBack this architecture makes it easy to provide a higher reliability of the network by providing backup links or redundancy in terms of components. Apart from that, even if a component fails in contrast to a typical GSM network communication in other parts of the network might be still available. For example, if the back-haul connection to a particular village breaks down VoIP/GSM calls within the village are still possible.

---

[1] http://www.openbts.org
[2] http://www.ettus.com/products

It should also be noted that the proposed architecture also allows for making VoIP calls with a normal computer like the OLPC laptop using a Soft-phone and the Wifi access network. The back-haul network transports both calls equally using the VoIP LSP.

Additionally the architecture allows for transparently changing of the actual transport protocol of the VoIP traffic. For example, in order to optimize the link utilization within the mesh instead of SIP the IAX2 protocol can be used which is able to aggregate the packets of multiple calls via a trunk connection, which leads to a larger packet size and therefore to a lower MAC overhead.

The OpenBTS software in combination with the USRP implements a so called nano-cell which has the advantage of low power consumption and low costs. The trade-off is the lower transmission power resulting in a smaller coverage area in comparison to a standard macro-cell, which is in-line with our target scenario which attempts to cover hot spots, i.e. smaller villages, but not the deserted areas between them.

Another approach would be to use commercial nano-cells like the ip.access nano-bts[5]. The advantage is the availability of ready to use devices. Currently the nano-bts is only supported by the OpenBSC project which tries to implement the ABIS1 protocol and all mandatory parts of the GSM architecture. This would increase the complexity of our mesh access points since they would be required to provide GSM functionality that is not required by our approach.

Both approaches allow building a minimal mesh node which only consists of a WLAN access point and a GSM access point which can be run on the same physical machine. A low power CPU like the Intel Atom is able to handle running the operation system, the OpenBTS module and the WiBack components.

As mentioned before nano-cells have a much smaller energy footprint in comparison with macro cells. Beneath the smaller energy consumption resulting of the smaller TX / RX amplification power can be saved by adapting the amplifier in times of low load which is more likely on a smaller cell. Additionally, lower power consumption leads to lower demand on cooling which again results in a lower power consumption of the entire system.

A standard GSM setup includes an Uninterruptible Power Supply (UPS) to power the base station in case of loss of power. An UPS setup consumes about 15% of the entire power required by the base station. Powering the nano-cell with solar and wind energy necessarily leads to a battery setup in order to buffer the energy which makes an additional UPS setup needless.

A usual macro-cell consumes between 1400W and 3700W depending on the number of carrier frequency used in the cell. A nano-cells instead consumes only between 30W and 60W depending on amplification and number of used carrier frequencies which makes a solar power supply realistic in particular in Africa due to the high solar irradiance.

3   Evaluation

In this section we evaluate the performance of our solution in an out-door testbed. First, we analyze the implemented scenario. Then we evaluate the possible impact of background traffic on prioritized VoIP flows and show that our traffic class based queueing can enforce the proper QoS assurance over five wireless hops.

3.1 Test Scenario

The test scenario, see Figure 3, has been setup using our wireless mesh testbed at the Fraunhofer Campus in Sankt Augustin, Germany[8]. The focus of this scenario is the evaluation of a WiBack network with OpenBTS-based access points for deployment in unconnected rural areas. The test setup consists of six mesh nodes, a gateway node, four forwarding nodes, as well as an access point node, which also incorporates the OpenBTS GSM module. The links between the nodes are implemented using standard IEEE 802.11 hardware in EDCA mode operating in the 5 GHz and the 700 MHz spectrum. The distances between between the nodes are between 20m and 50m, with the 700 MHz link being a None Line of Sight (NLOS) link. As depicted in Figure 3, the links are operating at different data rates. We have chosen a combination of sub-optimal real-world links to best match a realistic deployment scenario.

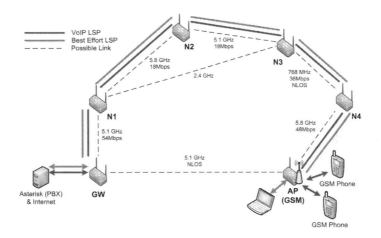

Fig. 3. Traffic is forwarded over four 5GHz and one 768 MHz WLAN Links

Our implementation is based on our high-performance C++ Simple and Extensible Network Framework (SENF)[5] which heavily utilizes boost[6] and modern C++ concepts. The MPLS forwarding function includes a monitoring component which allows us to examine the bandwidth, loss and delay figures per LSP. The figures obtained from this monitoring module will be used in the following sections.

3.2 Evaluation of the Standard Configuration

In the standard configuration, two separate LSP pairs have been configured between the GW and the AP node, one for the VoIP traffic and one for *best effort* traffic, see Figure 3. The Asterisk PBX is located behind the GW node and communicates with the OpenBTS component, which is located at the AP, via the VoIP LSP using SIP/RTP. No traffic aggregation is performed, hence each VoIP packet is sent independently.

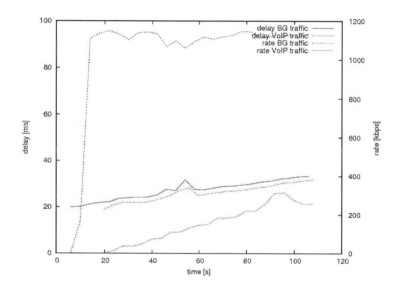

Fig. 4. Bandwidth and delay over an increasing number of phone calls

For this measurement we have loaded the best effort LSP with roughly 1100 kbps of Internet Control Message Protocol (ICMP) traffic. Then, approximately every ten seconds, we have established a new phone call using mobile phones. Figure 4 depicts the measured results on the upstream LSPs from the AP to the GW. The end-to-end latency on both LSPs increases linearly with the increasing load but remains below an acceptable limit for voice calls. No packet loss was observed on either LSP. Hence, we can show that, on not overloaded links, VoIP and best effort traffic can be carried in parallel.

3.3 Loaded Links and DiffServ

In this measurement we evaluated the performance of our architecture under highly loaded link conditions in order to verify that the forwarding function prioritizes the VoIP calls to still provide the committed QoS handling.

To simulate random background traffic, the *best effort* LSP was loaded with traffic generated by parallel *flood pings* with a packet size of 64, 128, 256, 512,

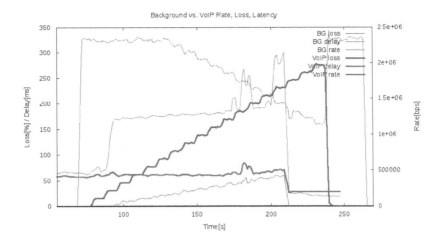

Fig. 5. Bandwidth, delay and loss of the *best effort* and VoIP LSPs under high load

1024 and 1450 bytes, respectively. As depicted in Figure 5, the accumulated background traffic mix added up to roughly 2.3Mbps. Every ten seconds an additional 64kbps VoIP call was added to the prioritized VoIP LSP, up to a maximum of 18 calls. Then all VoIP calls were terminated at time t=240s.

The thick lines in the figure, represent the data of the VoIP flows, while the thin lines represent the best efforts flow's data. It can be observed that initially the background traffic is carried smoothly across the mesh. With an increasing amount of VoIP flows, the bandwidth (blue) of the best effort flow decreases while its loss rate (red) and delay (green) increase accordingly. The VoIP LSP does not experience any increase of delay or noticeable loss.

4   Conclusion and Future Work

We have presented our solution to integrate a GSM nano-cell into WiBack, our meshed wireless back-haul network architecture. Using empirical measurements in our testbed we have shown that the VoIP traffic can be forwarded along a path consisting of five IEEE 802.11 based links without any major delay or loss. Even under high load situations, prioritized VoIP traffic was forwarded smoothly without any noticeable increase of loss or delay, well within the committed QoS assurances.

Future work will focus on the evaluation of trunking VoIP calls between the AP and the GW in order to lower the channel resource utilization overhead caused by the rather small VoIP packet on 802.11 links. Furthermore, we plan to extend to multimedia capability of our architecture by integration multicast-based services to support, for example, emergency paging or community radios.

Acknowledgment. The research leading to these results has received funding from the European Community's Seventh Framework Programme (FP7/2007-2013) under grant agreement n° 214994.

References

[1] Awduche, D., Berger, L., Gan, D., Li, T., Srinivasan, V., Swallow, G.: RSVP-TE: Extensions to RSVP for LSP Tunnels. RFC 3209 (Proposed Standard) (December 2001), Updated by RFCs 3936, 4420, 4874, 5151, 5420

[2] Awduche, D., Chiu, A., Elwalid, A., Widjaja, I., Xiao, X.: Overview and Principles of Internet Traffic Engineering. RFC 3272 (Informational) (May 2002), Updated by RFC 5462

[3] Banchs, A., Bayer, N., Chieng, D., de la Oliva, A., Gloss, B., Kretschmer, M., Murphy, S., Natkaniec, M., Zdarsky, F.: Carmen: Delivering carrier grade services over wireless mesh networks. In: Proc. IEEE 19th International Symposium on Personal, Indoor and Mobile Radio Communications PIMRC 2008, September 15-18, pp. 1–6 (2008)

[4] Farrel, A., Vasseur, J.-P., Ash, J.: A Path Computation Element (PCE)-Based Architecture. RFC 4655 (Informational) (August 2006)

[5] http://senf.berlios.de (accessed April 22, 2009)

[6] http://www.boost.org/ (accessed July 17, 2009)

[7] Kretschmer, M., Niephaus, C., Ghinea, G.: QoS-aware flow monitoring and event creation in heterogeneous MPLS-based wireless mesh networks supporting unidirectional links. In: 9th IEEE Malaysia International Conference on Communications 2009, Kuala Lumpur, Malaysia (2009)

[8] Kretschmer, M., Robitzsch, S., Niephaus, C., Jonas, K., Ghinea, G.: Wireless mesh network coverage with QoS differentiation for rural areas. In: First International Workshop on Wireless Broadband Access for Communities and Rural Developing Regions, Karlstad, Sweden (December 2008)

[9] Guy, E., Miller, F., Shumard, K., Spencer, M., Capouch, B.: Iax: Inter-asterisk exchange version 2. RFC 5456 (Informational) (Feburary 2010)

[10] Rosen, E., Tappan, D., Fedorkow, G., Rekhter, Y., Farinacci, D., Li, T., Conta, A.: MPLS Label Stack Encoding. RFC 3032 (Proposed Standard) (January 2001), Updated by RFCs 3443, 4182, 5332, 3270, 5129, 5462, 5586

[11] Rosen, E., Viswanathan, A., Callon, R.: Multiprotocol Label Switching Architecture. RFC 3031 (Proposed Standard) (January 2001)

[12] Rosenberg, J., Schulzrinne, H., Camarillo, G., Johnston, A., Peterson, J., Sparks, R., Handley, M., Schooler, E.: SIP: Session Initiation Protocol. RFC 3261 (Proposed Standard) (June 2002), Updated by RFCs 3265, 3853, 4320, 4916, 5393, 5621, 5626, 5630

[13] Schulzrinne, H., Casner, S., Frederick, R., Jacobson, V.: RTP: A Transport Protocol for Real-Time Applications. RFC 3550 (Standard) (July 2003), Updated by RFC 5506

Leveraging SMS Infrastructure for Internet Access in Developing Countries: Scenarios, Architecture and Research Directions

Fatna Belqasmi[1], Carl Aniambossou[2], and Roch Glitho[3]

[1] ETS, University of Quebec, Montreal, Canada
fbelqasmi@alumi.concordia.ca
[2] IMSP, University of Abomey Calavi, Republic of Benin
aniamss@gmail.com
[3] ETS, University of Quebec, & Concordia university, Canada
glitho@ece.concordia.ca

Abstract. Short message service (SMS) is now pervasive in many developing countries, thanks to the large footprint of second generation cellular systems, especially GSM. However, in many of these countries, only a handful of privileged end-users have Internet access. This state of affairs is a major impediment to the wide deployment of e-services, since most e-services require Internet access, and so has created a strong motivation for leveraging SMS infrastructure to enable Internet access for e-services in developing countries. This paper introduces real life scenarios, proposes an architecture and discusses the related research issues. The scenarios show that near-real time and even delayed access may be sufficient for many e-services – an option that has been used as the premise upon which the architecture relies. The kiosks are its pillars. They mediate between the widely deployed SMS service and the scarcely available Internet access. Related research issues are identified and discussed. Related work is also summarized.

Keywords: SMS, Internet access, networking for developing countries, e-services.

1 Introduction

Second generation cellular networks, especially Global System for Mobile communications (GSM), have very high growth and penetration rates in most developing countries. In the Republic of Benin (West Africa) for example, the number of GSM Subscriber Identity Module (SIM) cards sold in a year has grown from a couple of thousand in 2000 to close to 4 million in 2008, for a population of around 8 million [1]. The figures are staggering, even if we take into account the fact that a single individual in Benin may own up to five SIM cards at one time (i.e. a SIM card for each of the five different cellular networks in operation in the country) due to the high cost of inter-cellular networks calls.

R. Popescu-Zeletin et al. (Eds.): AFRICOMM 2010, LNICST 64, pp. 11–21, 2011.

This brings the GSM penetration rate to somewhere between 10% and 50%, most probably closer to 50% than 10% since only the well-to-do own several SIM cards. Most other people have either a single SIM card or a maximum of two. On the other hand, the current penetration rate for the Internet is at around 1.8% [2].

Electronic services (E-services) refer to the provisioning of services over the Internet (e.g. e-commerce, e-government). While they can potentially play a key role in most developing countries, the low Internet penetration rate remains a major impediment to their deployment.

On the other hand, short message service (SMS) is ubiquitous in these countries since it now comes as a basic service with GSM offerings. This situation creates the problematic of leveraging SMS infrastructure to enable Internet access for e-services in developing countries – the objective of this paper.

The next section presents real life scenarios. We assume the presence of a functional entity called a kiosk. Although the scenarios are from the specific context of Benin, they clearly illustrate the problematic and similar scenarios are commonly found in most other developing countries. The third section introduces the architecture we propose for the kiosk, and is followed by a discussion of, research directions and related work. We conclude in the last section.

2 Scenarios

Fig. 1 sets the stage. It depicts end-users with cellular phones and SMS access interacting with a kiosk that acts as a mediator between these users and an application server (AS) that is accessible via the Internet and that provides e-services.

The kiosk can either have permanent or intermittent connection to the Internet, or there may even be no connection. In the latter case, a mobile access point can be used to connect the kiosk to the Internet, as discussed in [3]. The access point could be connected to a public bus that moves between the kiosk's location and another kiosk

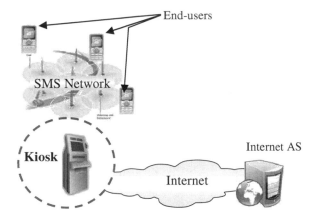

Fig. 1. Accessing Internet services via SMS

(K2) or a neighbouring city with Internet connection. The access point collects the pending requests from the kiosk, delivers them to K2 and gets the responses, and delivers these responses to the first kiosk the next time it gets close enough to it.

An online student registration system, an e-government and an e-banking system are discussed in this section.

2.1 On-line Student Registration

An on-line student registration system was recently launched in Benin to allow students to register for the academic year without having to physically go to the campus. The details of the system are presented below, including how a potential kiosk may make the usage ubiquitous.

To register, the students need to provide a set of information (by filling in a web form), including the student's name, marital status, phone number, email, and birthday, the school name, the major, and the year.

Students with real time Internet access can go on-line and register. However, to meet the needs of students with no real time Internet access, but who do have access to a cellular network that offers basic services such as SMS, an SMS-based registration e-service can be provided as follows (Fig. 2). We assume that the kiosk has a permanent Internet connection. However, cases with intermittent or no connection are also possible.

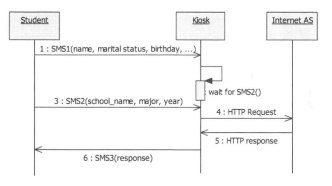

Fig. 2. SMS-based registration e-service

The student sends an SMS message to the kiosk with the required information. Due to the constraints on the SMS message length, the information may be sent in one or more SMS messages. We assume that two messages are required for this service. When the two messages are received, the kiosk creates an Internet/HyperText Transfer Protocol (HTTP) request which it will then send to the Internet AS. When a response is received, the kiosk maps the response into an SMS message that it sends to the students.

2.2 E-Government

There is currently no e-service for passport handling in Benin, although an e-service would significantly increase efficiency. The details of a potential e-service that will increase efficiency are presented below along with a potential kiosk that may aid in making the use pervasive.

Currently, to apply for a passport, applicants must travel to the passport service office in the city of Cotonou. When a request is filed, the applicant receives a receipt that has a unique number. The receipt will be used to track the level of evolution of the demand. Applicants need to continuously monitor the status of their applications, in order to get the passport in a reasonable amount of time (e.g. to avoid delays due to missing documents). The only way to obtain any tracking information is to insert the receipt into one of the reading machines available at the passport office. This procedure may result in applicants having to travel for several kilometres only to determine that their passport is not yet ready.

Sending an SMS to query the application status is much more convenient, easier, and less expensive. Furthermore, the response does not need to be sent in real time.

The e-government service can be supplied via SMS as follows: The applicant sends an SMS message to the kiosk with the receipt number. The kiosk sends an Internet request to a passport AS that will inform the kiosk about the current status of the application (e.g. documents missing, being processed, or passport ready). The kiosk forwards the status to the applicant in an SMS message. The passport AS may be provided by the passport office. It accesses the office's local database in order to consult the status of passport applications.

2.3 E-Banking

Some banks in Benin offer e-banking services. We present below a concrete example of an e-banking service offered by a local bank and show how, as in the previous scenarios, the kiosk may help in making e-banking services ubiquitous.

The e-banking service allows bank clients to execute a set of banking operations online. These include balance checking, viewing the last transaction, and transfers between accounts. Before a client can perform any of these operations, he or she must login using one of the access levels supported by the e-service: 'username/password' that provides basic access for viewing operations, 'digipass' that allows for transfers between accounts, and 'DigipassGO3 for a higher security level.

In this scenario, near real time access or even delayed Internet access may be sufficient for most clients (especially for viewing operations). We assume therefore that the kiosk has intermittent Internet connection. The SMS-based e-banking can work as follows: The client sends an SMS message to the kiosk with the login level and information, and the requested banking operation. The kiosk saves the message locally and replies back with an SMS message confirming the request reception. When an Internet connection becomes available, the kiosk sends the corresponding HTTP request and forwards the response back to the client.

3 Proposed Architecture

Several requirements can be derived from the scenarios above, and they are discussed next. The architectural building blocks that make the kiosk are then presented. We end the section by an illustrative scenario.

3.1 Requirements

The first requirement is that the kiosk should be accessible via both SMS and the Internet. This will enable the end-users/kiosks to send their requests using SMS/Internet, and all the Internet ASs to reply via the Internet.

Second, the kiosk should handle requests in which more than one SMS message is needed to create the corresponding Internet request. This is required for many e-service applications, such as the on-line student registration scenario presented earlier.

Third, the kiosk should support all forms of internet access, including real-time, intermittent and no access. It should also allow the use of the same e-service applications via any of the access forms (e.g. as discussed in the e-banking scenario). This will allow the kiosk to be deployed in different environments, ranging from a big city with real-time Internet access to a small and distant village with no access.

Fourth, in cases where a kiosk has no Internet access, the existing access infrastructures (e.g. GSM, wireless/WiFi) should be used to (temporarily) connect the kiosk to the Internet, and so no new access infrastructure should need to be deployed.

Fifth, in order to be able to handle requests in situations with intermittent or no Internet access, the kiosk should support a store and forward mechanism and therefore provide a storage capability (software and hardware).

Sixth, the kiosk should be scalable in terms of the end-users to be supported; allowing for the handling of more than one end-user at a time and for more than one request initiated by a single end-user.

The last requirement is security. The key features to be addressed are authentication and authorization, confidentiality, and non-repudiation. In the banking scenario, for instance, the end-user should be authenticated and he/she should be able to execute only the operations he/she is allowed to (e.g. an end-user should not transfer money from an account for which he has no authority). Furthermore, the username and password sent for login should be kept strictly confidential

3.2 Architectural Building Blocks

Fig. 3 depicts the architectural building blocks of the kiosk. The kiosk application includes the logic needed for processing incoming SMS requests, and for coordinating the work of the other building blocks. The SMS message handler (SMH) processes received SMS messages (i.e. extract the message content, formats it in a way that the application can understand, and transmits it to the application). It also creates and sends new SMS messages using the SMS access module (SAM). The Internet message handler (IMH) creates and sends new Internet requests and processes received Internet responses. The Internet access module (IAM) handles intermittent and occasional (i.e. only available on some occasions, such as when a mobile access point is in range) connections, and stores and forwards outgoing messages according to the access availability. The SAM can also store and forward SMS messages when there is an intermittent (or occasionally unavailable) SMS connection.

The kiosk supports two types of e-services: customized and non-customized. Each customized e-service is given a unique identifier (ID). The kiosk maintains a mapping between the ID and the associated service address (i.e. the Uniform Resource Identifier -URI). The kiosk also keeps the list of the information required by the e-service to handle a specific request (e.g. a receipt number is required to get the passport application status), and the number of the SMS messages required. The SMS requests need to include the target e-service ID.

For non-customized e-services, no information is kept by the kiosk. The end-user sends the service URI as part of the request SMS.

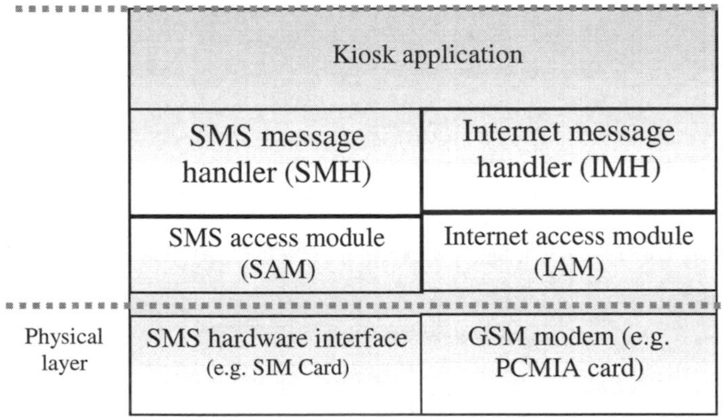

Kiosk application	
SMS message handler (SMH)	Internet message handler (IMH)
SMS access module (SAM)	Internet access module (IAM)
SMS hardware interface (e.g. SIM Card)	GSM modem (e.g. PCMIA card)

Physical layer

Fig. 3. Overall architecture of the kiosk building blocks

3.2.1 Kiosk Application

When the application receives an SMS request, the request begins in the 'Session Manager' module, that spawns a new 'Session Agent' to handle the request (Fig. 4). In order to support requests from different end-users at the same time, as well as many requests from a single end-user, each session agent is associated to the telephone number from which the SMS request was received and the identifier of the request. The "E-service information database" stores the customized services' information.

To process a request for a customized service, the agent first verifies the number of SMS messages needed and then waits until all of the messages are received or a configurable timeout expires. After all of the messages are received, the agent checks the information received in these messages against that on the database to verify if all of the information needed by the e-service has been provided. If this is not the case, the agent informs the end-user via a response SMS. The agent may give hints about what is missing. The information verification at the kiosk side will optimize the response time, as opposed to the alternative, where the verification is only done on the e-service side (which may take several hours or days).

After a successful verification, the agent calls the appropriate function on the IMH, which creates and sends the corresponding Internet request. When a response is received from the e-service, the agent uses the SMH to map the response to an SMS message and sends it to the end-user.

For non-customized e-services, the received request SMS is directly mapped to an Internet request and sent out.

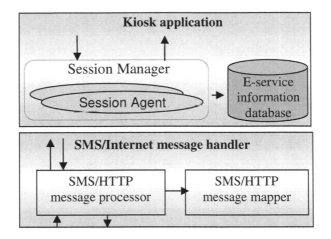

Fig. 4. Architecture of the kiosk application and the SMS/Internet message handler

3.2.2 SMS/Internet Message Handler
The architecture of the SMH and the IMH is shown in Fig. 4. Each handler includes a message processor and a message mapper. When a message arrives for the handler, it is received by the message processor.

When the 'SMS message processor' receives a request, it extracts its content and forwards it to the application. When a response arrives, the processor uses the 'SMS message mapper' to map the response to an SMS message and then sends it to the destination.

Regarding the 'HTTP message processor', when it is asked to send a request, it uses the 'HTTP message mapper' to create the request using the information received from the application, and then it sends the request. The response's content is extracted and forwarded to the application.

3.2.3 Internet Access Module
Fig. 5 depicts the IAM architecture. The messages that need to be sent arrive ate the 'access manager' module. If an Internet access is available, the messages are sent directly to their destination. Otherwise, the manager asks the application (via the message handler) to send a provisional response to the end-user and stores the messages in the 'temporary storage database- TSD'. The TSD also maintains information about the order in which the messages are stored.

The next time Internet access is re-established, this will be detected by the 'Access detector' that will inform the 'message sender'. The latter will then consult the TSD, get the messages waiting for transmission, and sends them out following first-in-first-out algorithm. The arriving messages (i.e. responses) are received by the 'message receiver' and forwarded to the 'Internet Message handler' via the 'access manager'.

The SAM has a similar architecture and it functions in a similar way, except that the request and response processing are reversed. Indeed, the requests are forwarded to the upper layer and the responses are stored if the SMS access is unavailable.

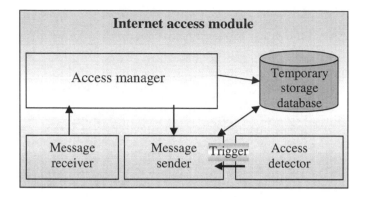

Fig. 5. Architecture of the Internet Access Module

3.3 Illustrative Scenario

Fig. 6 presents the sequence diagram for an end-user requesting the status of their passport application. The end-user sends an SMS request with the passport e-service ID and the receipt number to the kiosk. The request is received by the SAM, which forwards it to the SMH. The SMH processes the message and transmits the formatted message to the kiosk application. The kiosk application checks that the e-service only needs one SMS message, verifies that all the information needed by the e-service has been provided, gets the target URI, and asks the IMH to send a corresponding Internet request. The handler maps the formatted message into an appropriate request and instructs the IAM to send the request. The access module verifies the Internet access availability and sends the request. The response is forwarded back to the end-user following the reverse path of the request.

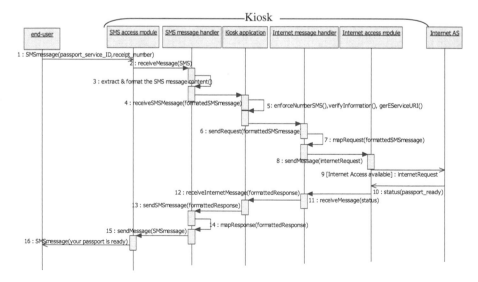

Fig. 6. Scenario sequence diagram

4 Research Directions and Related Work

4.1 Research Directions

The first research direction related to SMS-based e-services is that of a business model. The owner of the kiosk should be identified, and the relationships/interactions (e.g. inter-working for service provisioning, compensation) with the other involved operators (e.g. GSM network provider, Internet AS provider, mobile access point provider) should be specified. For instance, the owner could be a third party or one of the existing operators.

The second direction is session management. In the e-banking scenario, for example, the end-user must login before sending any banking operation request. The login and banking operation require two separate but inter-related Internet requests. The Internet AS accepts the second request only after the first has been executed successfully. The challenge is how to send and execute these two requests when a kiosk may have no Internet access. We cannot afford to wait for the login response before we send the banking request, because the delay between the two may be too long and the session at the AS side may expire before the second request can be received.

Another session-related challenge is how is the session managed at the kiosk side? For instance, how long can a kiosk keep a delayed session (in a case no Internet access) open, before it notifies the client that the request cannot be fulfilled, or to resend the request? Some general patterns may be defined to optimize the session management, depending, for example, on the Internet access behavior (e.g. intermittent, occasional, and periodic).

The third research direction is in routing. In cases with only occasional Internet access, for instance, there may be no route towards the destination when the SMS request is received. The challenge is how to detect a route whenever it becomes available and how to forward the responses back to the source (when a response is created, the route used by the request may no longer be usable). Routing in delay-tolerant networks (DTNs) is one potential approach [4]. DTNs are networks characterized by long delay paths and frequent network partitions [6].

The fourth direction is concrete realization of the kiosk architecture. Existing potential approaches should be analyzed and the more appropriate alternative identified. A centralized approach where all of the kiosk architectural building blocks are deployed in the same box may make kiosk deployment and management easier. The distributed approach with the building blocks in different boxes and well-defined reference points between the blocks may be more scalable, but requires more management effort. Indeed, in addition to managing each box separately, the connections between the boxes should also be managed. Furthermore, the inter-boxes communication may introduce more delays.

The last research direction is security. The end-users should be authenticated, authorization policies applied, and message integrity ensured end-to-end (i.e. between the end-user and the Internet AS) and on the kiosk side. In addition, the messages' confidentiality should also be maintained while the messages travel between nodes. This includes the time when the messages are stored by the kiosk or by intermediary nodes.

4.2 Related Work

We categorize the related work into two classes: related to e-service provisioning via SMS, and related to delayed/asynchronous e-service access. The work discussed in reference [5] falls in the first class, and compares several ways for providing e-services in emerging markets using cell phones, including SMS. The end-users send an SMS to the e-service number with appropriate keywords, and get back the answer via SMS. End-users can also subscribe to an e-service (e.g. weather forecast) and get periodic notifications.

The same paper also discusses the strengths and weaknesses of SMS-based e-services. Strengths include ease of use by end-users, availability on all phones, low network requirements (SMS does not need high bandwidth networks), and low and predictable cost. The weaknesses are mainly related to the illiteracy of emerging countries' populations, the limited input capabilities of mobile phones, and the lack of standardization for SMS-based application development.

However, reference [5] does not discuss the actual architecture to use, nor how the actual services are or can be implemented.

Examples of related work in the second class (i.e. related to delayed e-service access) include the Saami Network Connectivity (SNC) project and the DakNet network. The SNC project [8] aims to provide Internet access to the Saami population of reindeer herders in Swedish Lapland, who relocate many times a year following the natural behavior of reindeer. To allow access to e-services in SNC, each remote area is set as a Network Address Translation (NAT) zone. An application layer gateway is placed at the edge of each zone, in order to terminate the Internet requests and produce outgoing bundles. A bundle encompasses all the information required to complete an Internet action. The data bundles are relayed between gateways using DTN routing [4] through a series of fixed and mobile relay caches.

DakNet was designed to provide Internet access to outlying villages lacking digital communications. It transmits data over short point-to-point links between kiosk's mobile access points. These mobile access points can be mounted on a bus, a motorcycle, or even a bicycle with a small generator. They transport data among the kiosks and the Internet access points.

These two solutions reuse existing access infrastructures (e.g. GSM, WiFi, or satellite radio links) to provide Internet access. However, the kiosks in these solutions are not accessible via both SMS and the Internet, since they only provide Internet access. Furthermore, the requirement for the ability to handle requests where more than one SMS message is needed to create the corresponding Internet request is not relevant for these two systems.

5 Conclusions

This paper proposes an architecture for SMS-based e-services, in which an end-user sends an SMS request to a kiosk with the information the e-service needs, and the kiosk relies the request to the Internet AS. The information needed by the e-service may be sent using more than one SMS message. The kiosk supports different forms of Internet access. When the kiosk receives an SMS request, two alternatives are possible. If Internet access is available, the kiosk maps the SMS request to an Internet request that it sends to the target AS. When the kiosk receives a response, it creates an SMS out of the response content and sends it to the client. If no Internet access is available, the Internet request is stored at the kiosk until the access is recovered. The Internet request may pass through a number of intermediary nodes before it reaches the target AS (e.g. another kiosk, a moving connection point).

The paper also introduces real life scenarios and discusses the related research issues, including business models, session management, routing, kiosk realization and security, security – all of which will continue to be areas of our future research, along with extending the proposed architecture accordingly.

References

1. Autorité Transitoire de la Regulation des Postes et Telecommunicaions du Benin, Rapport d activités (2009), http://www.atrpt.bj//
2. Africa Internet Usage and Population Statistics, http://www.internetworldstats.com/stats1.htm
3. Pentland, A., Fletcher, R., Hasson, A.: DakNet: Rethinking Connectivity in Developing Nations. Computer 37(1), 78–83 (2004), doi:10.1109/MC.2004.1260729
4. Jain, S., Fall, K., Patra, R.: Routing in a delay tolerant network. ACM SIGCOMM Computer Communication 34(4), 145–158 (2004)
5. Boyera, S.: The Mobile Web to Bridge the Digital Divide? Paper presented at the IST-Africa Conference 2007, Maputo, Mozambique (2007)
6. Fall, K.: A delay-tolerant network architecture for challenged internets. In: Proceedings of the Conference on Applications, Technologies, Architectures, and Protocols for Computer Communications, pp. 27–34 (August 2003)
7. Biswas, S., Morris, R.: ExOR: opportunistic multi-hop routing for wireless networks. In: Proceedings of Conference on Applications, Technologies, Architectures, and Protocols for Computer Communications, pp. 133–144 (August 2005)
8. Doria, Uden, M., Pandey, D.P.: Providing connectivity to the Saami nomadic community. In: Proceedings of the Second International Conference on Open Collaborative Design for Sustainable Innovation (December 2002)

A Structural Parameter Based Modification of Energy Conscious ESPAR Antenna System through Optimization for WLAN's Dual-Band Operability

Mncedisi J. Bembe[1], Willem Clarke[2], and Albert A. Lysko[3]

[1] ITTP - Korean Advanced Institute of Technology
119 Munji-ro, Yusengong-gu, Daejeon, Republic of Korea
Mncedisie@gmail.com
[2] Department of Electrical and Electronic Engineering Science, University of Johannesburg,
P.O. Box 524, Auckland Park, 2006, South Africa
willemc@uj.ac.za
[3] CSIR Meraka Institute,
P.O. Box 395, Pretoria 0001, South Africa
ALysko@csir.co.za

Abstract. Phased array antenna's radiation pattern can be electronically controlled, making them a relevant solution for multipath interference. Electronically Steerable Parasitic Array Radiator (ESPAR) antenna systems are part of the family of phased array antennas under the umbrella of aerial beam-forming antennas. Generally ESPAR antenna system design considers the quarter wavelength approach. In practice there are a significant number of multiband systems with many applications integrated in a single device. This paper looks at the design of a dual-band ESPAR antenna. The design is limited to the ESPAR antenna's structural parameter modification through the loading of its element with inductance load (circuitry). This results in an antenna system which operates in both 2.4GHz and 5.8 GHz bands of the IEEE 802.11 WLAN (Wireless Local Area Network) suitable for rural areas. The approach employed in this work consists of different stages of structural modification with careful optimization processes. The two adopted process are the quarter wavelength design and the optimization process, conducted through the genetic optimization algorithm.

Keywords: ESPAR Antenna system, WLAN, Genetic Algorithm.

1   Introduction

The recent trends on development of wireless technologies show that wireless networks are faced with many challenges. This is due to an increasing user demand, limited radio resource, search for cost effective, long range devices and limited supply power resource [1]. This implies that service providers must search for new and effective ways to counter the above outlined obstacles. The increasing user demand requires a high transmission rate communication system. There are two main challenges for high transmission rate realization: multiple interferences and the multiple access interference

R. Popescu-Zeletin et al. (Eds.): AFRICOMM 2010, LNICST 64, pp. 22–30, 2011.

(MAI). One technique which addresses these impairments is the use of antenna array concurrently with effected detection scheme [2].

The question is: how can this antenna array be developed inexpensively and effectively for WLAN suitable for *open, rural areas* with minimum communication resources [3]? Earlier solutions which were adopted by operators include, with no limitation: tower-top amplifiers, high gain directional antennas and other available solutions. The challenge with these techniques is that they have a circuit complexity [4, 5]. One emerging technology is the Electronically Steerable Parasitic Array Radiator (ESPAR) antenna system. It is a hardware realization of the Aerial beam-forming antenna system. The configuration of the ESPAR antenna system consists of the following: one active monopole element and N reactive parasitic elements positioned near the active radiating element as depicted in FIG.1 [6, 7, and 8]. It is through this feature of using one active element that this antenna system is lower cost and energy efficient as compared to digital and microwave beam-forming which both have high fabrication cost and high energy consumption relative to the ESPAR [6]. The radiation pattern is steered in different directions using reactive loads and appropriate beamforming algorithms [9 and 10].

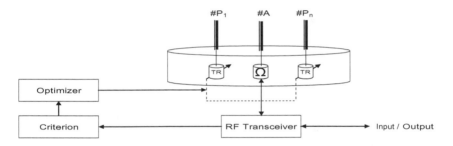

Fig. 1. A typical ESPAR antenna with N-number of ESPAR antenna

In this study the ESPAR antenna technique is adopted, its structural parameter is modified for IEEE 802.11a/b/g frequency bands. The main objective of the study is to develop a dual band ESPAR antenna which adopts cost effective techniques with low fabrication cost and is practical. The results expected are: (a) performance of allowed return loss value, (b) acceptable gain at the specified frequency bands (2.4GHz and 5.8GHz), and (c) by determining if the design of the antenna can be practically realized, while determining if it directs its beam with any variation in the combination of the reactance values.

2 Dual ESPAR Antenna Configuration

ESPAR design is classified into two groups, which are significantly important for the design of this antenna system. The two groups are [11]: Structural Parameters and the Control Parameter. Structural Parameters refer to the mechanical properties of the antenna, these are: N- number of the passive elements; the length of the active antenna l_o; the length of the parasitic elements l_n ($n=1$, $2...N$), where it is required that the length of all the passive elements be equal in order to achieve omni-directional pattern; the distance between the active and the passive elements d. The Control Parameter compose of the reactance X_n (n = 1, 2...N) , which are responsible for the control of the antenna's radiation pattern [12]. The scope of optimization is only limited to the structural parameters of the ESPAR antenna system, which is expected to satisfy the requirements of this study.

A basic configuration of ESPAR antenna system is composed of one active (fed) centre element surrounded by one or more elements not connected to RF directly (parasitic or passive elements). The main difference from the conventional phased array is that it uses one active fed element, and inter-element coupling with radiation mechanism is used for beam-forming and that the reactance devices are directly loaded to the ports of the parasitic elements. The centre element is the only element fed with RF signal, resulting in one transmitter / receiver front-end circuitry required. The bias voltage is always reverse to the varicap diode (variable reactance) used, meaning that very little DC current is used in the parasitic elements [13].

The literature shows that there are various types of design modification that can be conducted in order to enable it to operate in dual or multiple bands. These types includes: Fractals technology [13], RLC (Resistor, Inductor and capacitor circuit) loading [14], matching networks [15], etc.

In this work the RLC loading is considered. There are two approaches adopted for RLC loading, the conventional approach and an optimization-based approach [16]. The conversional approach is not efficient in terms of identifying the location and the magnitude of the loads.

The three challenges in loading the antenna are to identify the location(s) of the resonant circuits, define the component values and identify the resonant frequency for the prescribed frequency band. Optimization based RLC loading deals with a stochastic problem. Most popular tool used for these types of problems is the genetic algorithm (GA) [16]. GA operates on discrete and/or coded representation of the parameters which are to be optimized, but not directly on the parameters. Equation (1) shows the formula used to transform continuous parameters to chromosomes used for genetic algorithm.

$$X = X_{min} + \frac{X_{min} - X_{max}}{2^{N_v} - 1} \sum_{n=0}^{N^X - 1} b_n^X 2^n$$

(1)

N^X–is the bit string and b_0^X,..., b (N^X - 1) X is the binary representation of X. Then X_{max} and X_{min} are the maximum and the minimum allowed values for X [16].

3   Optimization Procedure

This section was treated with a step by step hierarchical approach, resulting to identifying the range of the load's magnitude, and the following step being the optimization of the length of the monopole antenna plus the loading optimization and lastly it was the optimization of the ESPAR antenna.

3.1   Reactance Range Definition

The initial step is to identify the range by running the inductance range from zero to 400 Henry against the reflection coefficient and then identify the deeps in the coefficient. A much narrower initial range could have been used, by considering a realizable range only. In this work a wide range was considered as it will give the reader a different perspective if a wide range of inductance was realizable. The range that has minimum deeps will be defined as the inductance range of consideration. The resulting reflection coefficient is shown in FIG.2. The reflection coefficients plots were made with respect to the two resonant frequencies (2.4GHz and 5.8GHz) per single location of load (six lines graph expected). The only varying component was the inductance which was restricted to this range of zero to 400 henries [16]. The result shows that minimum deeps are observed below 50nH and that at zero it will start to behave as a capacitor as it goes towards the negative capacitor range. The range of 0-50 nH is the interesting part of this work as it gives the minimum reflection coefficient with respect to the inductance loads on the antenna elements. The minimum obtained reflection coefficient values were as follows:

- 2.4 GHz (S11a = 0.25, S11b =0.92, S11c =0.25) and
- 5.8 GHz (S11d = 0.56, S11e = 0.0.25, S11f =0.64).

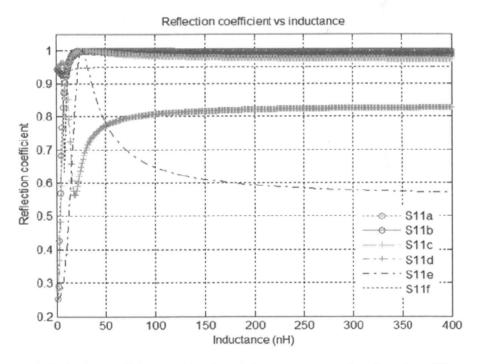

Fig. 2. Reflection coefficient resulting from inductance range conducted on three different locations on a monopole.

3.2 Monopole Antenna Optimization

This section focuses on both the length input parameter, which are the length of monopole and the effects of loading it through optimization. The following is the objective function used for the optimization of the loadings. The objective function (2) ignores the gain, which is a considered in the final stages of the work and the use of exponent five was done arbitrary for scaling purposes.

$$OF_a = |S_{11(2.4GHz)}|^5 + = |S_{11(2.4GHz)}|^5 .$$

$$(2)$$

The following stage is different compared to the inductance identifying stage. Different optimization process is conducted for the three different resonance frequencies (2.4GHz, 5.8GHz and the combination of the two frequencies). In this section, the theoretical monopole length was compared to the optimized length. In FIG.3 a depiction of a monopole antenna with three loadings as represented in (WIPLD) Wire Plate – Dielectric modeling tool. WIPLD is a software package tool, designed specifically for fast, accurate simulation and design of microwave circuits, devices and antennas [17]. The challenge in this section is to optimize the length of the parasitic elements and the loading to converge to the expected results both on gain and the return loss as the measure tool used for this work.

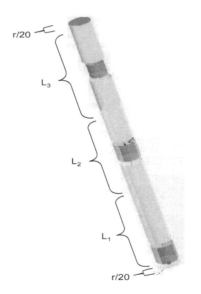

Fig. 3. Monopole antenna with three RLC loading

3.3   ESPAR Antenna Optimization

The number of elements used was varied from 3 to 7 elements, where the final number of elements used was 7 elements, because of the smooth switching that this number of element provides [18]. There are five input parameters included in TABLE I, which are the distance from the active element, the location of the loads, the number of loads, the loads value and the length of the parasitic element. This setup is such that the active element is fixed and the parasitic elements' distance from the active element and its length are optimized. The input parameters used are as follows: The distance range is from $0.2*\lambda_{5.8}$ to $1.3*\lambda_{5.8}$ and the height of the parasitic were ranged from $0.1*\lambda_{5.8}$ to $\lambda_{5.8}$ [19]. The loading was done in the following approach: Parasitic elements were kept as closed circuit while parasitic element one (P_1) was loaded with a reactance $Z = 1e9 + 1e9j\ \Omega$. The second scenario is to load P_2 while P_1 is also kept loaded; this was done until P_6, the reactance load value which was used for reflection is $Z = 1e9 + 1e9j\ \Omega$. The expected gain is 0 dB in the azimuthal direction and the Voltage Standing Wave Ratio (VSWR≤2).

Table 1. Input parameters for optimization process

Input Parameters	Minimum	maximum	Steps
N_l = Number of Loads (units)	≥ 1	≤ 3	1
L = Monopole length (m)	$\geq \lambda_{5.8GHz}/10$	$\leq \lambda_{5.8GHz}$	$0.05\ \lambda_{5.8GHz}$
L_1=load 1 location range (m)	$> r/20$	$\leq L/3$	$\dfrac{\left(\frac{L}{3}-\frac{r}{20}\right)}{32}$
L_2=load 2 location range (m)	$> L/3$	$\leq L/1.5$	$\dfrac{\left(\frac{L}{1.5}-\frac{L}{3}\right)}{32}$
L_3=load 3 location range (m)	$> L/1.5$	$\leq L-(r/20)$	$\dfrac{\left(\left(L-\left(\frac{r}{20}\right)\right)-\frac{L}{1.5}\right)}{32}$
L_{v1} = The range value of load 1(nH)	≥ 0	≤ 100	0.1 nH
L_{v2} = The range value of load 1(nH)	≥ 0	≤ 100	0.1 nH
L_{v3} = The range value of load 1(nH)	≥ 0	≤ 100	0.1 nH
d_p = distance from active element	$\geq 0.2*\lambda_{5.8}$	$\leq 1.3*\lambda_{5.8}$	$0.05*\lambda_{5.8}$
h_p = parasitic element's height	$\geq 0.1*\lambda_{5.8}$	$\leq \lambda_{5.8}$	$0.05*\lambda_{5.8}$

4 Simulation Results

The simulation process was conducted with the consideration of the input parameters shown in TABLE 1 and the procedures described in the previous section. Fig.4 Shows one of the final configuration which was optimized.

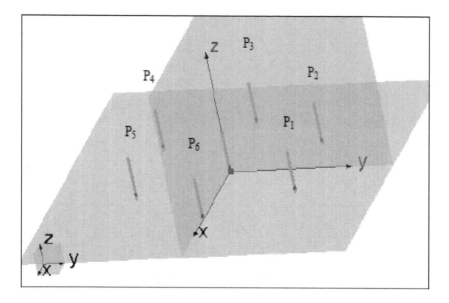

Fig. 4. The configuration of the ESPAR antenna system

The following diagram in FIG.5 shows the gain which is about 4 dB for the 2.4 GHz and 8dB for the 5.8 GHz in omni-directional pattern.

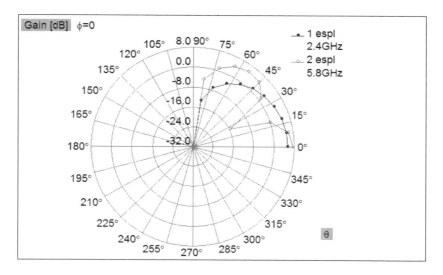

Fig. 5. The elevation gain of the ESPAR antenna using the spherical view

The last result shown is the standing voltage wave ratio (SVWR) or the return loss. The return loss is depicted in FIG.6, with the magnitude of -8 dB and -9.6 dB for both 2.4 GHz and the 5.8 GHz respectively.

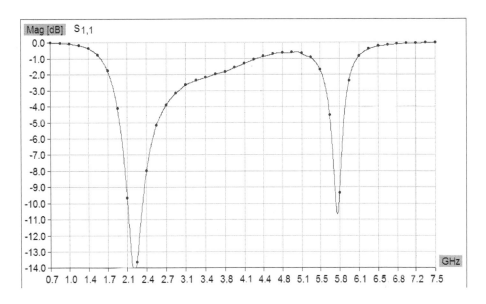

Fig. 6. The return loss for the ESPAR antenna which has shown improvement with respect to the optimization

5 Conclusion

This work has achieved the integration of ESPAR antenna system with loading technique. This is traditionally observed on wire antenna without being adopted for smart antennas systems, but if it is adopted it is extended to reactance parameter. In this study the optimization is only limited to structural parameters. The dual band ESPAR antenna was design with simulation results showing -8 dB and -9.4 dB in both 2.4 GHz and 5.8 GHz frequency bands. The only challenge which was encountered was on the steering capabilities which were limited for three different separated optimization processes with three separate different conditions. Investigations are conducted ensure acceptable pattern steering maintains the same return loss for the omni-directional ESPAR antenna. The investigation is in different stages. The genetic algorithm was used in three stages through the scope of the structural based optimization. The three stages involve monopole length antenna its loading and the ESPAR antenna optimization.

References

1. Bembe, M.J., Lysko, A.A., Nyandeni, T.C., Clarke, W.A.: Design of Energy Conscious Antenna System for WLAN Frequency Band. In: SATNAC (2009)
2. Islam, M.I., Gaus, M.G., Das, A., Sarkar, M.U., Amin, M.R.: Adaptive array antenna system in cancellation of jammer and noise of wireless link. In: 12th Int'l. Conference on Computers and Information Technology, pp. 321–326 (December 2009)

3. Ntsibane, N.: Energy Efficient wireless mesh networks, Wireless World Research Forum. In: SATNAC (2007)
4. Rayal, F.: Why have smart antennas not yet gained traction with wireless network operators? IEEE Antennas and Propagation Magazine 47, 124–126 (2005)
5. Wireless Africa, http://www.meraka.org.za/wireless.htm (referenced on the February 15, 2010)
6. Ohira, T., Iigusa, K.: Electronically Steerable Parasitic Array Radiator. The Institute of Electronics, Information and Communication Engineers 87, 12–31 (2004)
7. Harrington, R.: Reactively Controlled Antenna Arrays. IEEE Trans. Antennas & Propagat. 14, 62–65 (2003)
8. Parnes, M.D., Vendik, O.G., Korolkov, V.D.: Design of a Steerable Reflect-array Antenna with Semiconductor Tunable Varactor Diodes. Progress in Electromagnetics Research Symposium (March 2006)
9. Park, C., Takada, J., Sakaguchi, K., Ohira, T.: Analysis of a Radial-Cavity-Excited ESPAR Antenna. IEIC Technical Report 103, 17–20 (2003)
10. Schaer, B., Rambabu, K., Bornemann, J., Vahldieck, R.: Design of reactive parasitic elements in electronic beam steering arrays. IEEE Trans. Antennas & Propagat. 53, 1998–2003 (2005)
11. Ojiro, Y., Kawakami, H., Ohira, T., Gyoda, K.: Imporvement of Elevation Directivity for ESPAR Antenna with finite Ground Plane. IEEE Trans. Antenna and Propagat. 4, 18–21 (2001)
12. Gyoda, K., Ohira, T.: Design of electronically steerable passive array radiator (ESPAR)antennas. In: IEEE Antennas and Propagation Society International Symposium, vol. 2, pp. 922–925 (2000)
13. Tsachtsiris, G.F., Soras, C.F., Karaboikis, M.P., Makios, V.T.: Analysis of a modified Sierpinski Gasket monopole antenna printed on dual band wireless devices. IEEE Transactions on Antennas and Propagation 52, 2571–2579 (2004)
14. Boag, A., Michielssen, E., Mittra, R.: Design of Electrically Loaded Wire Antennas Using Genetic Algorithms. IEEE Trans. Antennas and Propagat. 44, 687–695 (1996)
15. Balanis, C.A.: Antenna Theory- Analysis and Design, 3rd edn. John Wiley and Sons, Chichester (2005)
16. Boag, A., Michielssen, E., Mittra, R.: Design of Electrically Loaded Wire Antennas Using Genetic Algorithms. IEEE Trans. Antennas and Propagat. 44, 687–695 (1996)
17. Kolundzija, B., Ognjanovic, J., Sarkar, T., Harrington, R.: WIPL: a program for electromagnetic modeling of composite-wire andplate structures. IEEE Antennas and Propagation Magazine 38, 75–79 (1996)
18. Taromaru, M., Ohira, T.: Electronically Steerable Parasitic Array Radiator Antenna – Principle, Control Theory and Its Application. In: Proc. Int. Union of Radio Science General Assembly, New Dehli, India (October 2005)
19. Shibata, O., Furuhi, T.: Dual-band ESPAR antenna for wireless LAN applications. IEEE Trans. Antennas and Propagat. 2B, 605–608 (2005)

Continent-Based Comparative Study of Internet Attacks

Idris A. Rai and Matsiko Perez

Makerere University, Kampala, Uganda
rai@cit.mak.ac.ug, mushura.perez@gmail.com

Abstract. We have deployed a honeypot sensor node in Uganda that is connected to a distributed honeypot system managed by Leurrecom.org Honeypot project, which constitutes of a large number of different *honeypot* sensors distributed across different continents. Once joined the project, the system allows access to the whole dataset collected by all sensors in the distributed system. We use the data collected by the honeypot sensors for a period of six months to compare the attacks that have been detected by honeypot sensors in Africa to the attacks detected by sensors in other continents. Our findings reveals that sensor nodes in Africa experience a significant number of attacks. In some cases, the number of attacks for African sensor nodes is significantly higher than many sensors in developed countries. This shows that network attacks are independent of location and Internet popularity in a country. That is, low Internet penetration level in African countries does not mean that networks in Africa are safe from external attacks. In fact, the results further indicate that some attacks are highly likely guided against specific networks.

Keywords: Internet attacks, threats, honeypot sensor, distributed honeypot systems, SGNET.

1 Introduction

In order to effectively protect the Internet, there is a need to have an indepth knowledge of Internet threats and attacks. To achieve this, it is very necessary to collect sound measurements about the existing and emerging Internet threats and their processes as observed on the Internet world over. Several initiatives have been in existence to monitor malicious activities or to capture malware information [1, 2, 10, 12, 13, 14]. In this paper we use one of the most recent similar initiative called Leurrecom.org project and its data collection infrastructure using SGNET deployment to study Internet attacks [4]. Leurrecom project is based on worldwide distributed system of *honeypot sensors* that are deployed in more than 30 countries covering five continents. The major objective of the project is to have a clear knowledge of the nature and behaviors of threats/attacks happening on the Internet by collecting data on the attacks on a long term perspective.

A *honeypot sensor* can be defined as a security resource whose value lies in being probed, attacked, or compromised [3]. The concept of honeypot was

R. Popescu-Zeletin et al. (Eds.): AFRICOMM 2010, LNICST 64, pp. 31–40, 2011.

introduced by L. Spitzner [3] in the late 1990's with the main goal of studying attacks/threats and their trends on a global scale across the whole Internet. In this paper, we will refer to a honeypot sensor as a *sensor*.

SGNET honeypot technology that is used in Leurrecom project differs from other honeypot systems in that it coordinates honeypot sensors and seamlessly integrates them into a distributed architecture through an overlay based on ad-hoc HTTP-like protocol called Peiros. The result of this integration is a distributed honeypot deployment that is able to automatically learn and handle server-based exploits, and emulate the code injection attacks up to the point of the malware download [15]. Leurrecom project uses ScriptGen technology to collect data from all sensors. In this paper, we use SGNET to investigate Internet attacks at continental level. We are specifically interested in comparing the nature of the attacks experienced by honeypot sensors in Africa to sensors in other continents.

Inspite of the existence of a few sub-marine cable initiatives to connect networks in developing countries to the Internet, most networks in Africa, mainly Sub-Saharan Africa are still connected to the Internet using low-speed satellite links. As a result, access to Internet is still not affordable to many, leading to stagnant or low Internet penetration in African countries. In turn, Internet traffic dynamics in developing countries are very simple and fairly predictable compared to traffic patterns in developed countries. As such, attackers might, perhaps rightfully, assume that the lack of wide spread Internet access in African countries is synonymous to lack of Internet security awareness and security expertise to secure and troubleshoot the networks. Others Africa might well think that attackers wouldn't be interested in simple networks in Africa. While the former is a very good motivation for attackers to test their newly developed attacks, we show that the later belief is practically very wrong and misleading.

We use the data gathered by all active sensors on Leurrecom project for a period of six months, mainly from Dec 2009 to May 2010. The analysis of the data reveals that the honeypot sensors in Africa experience a significant amount of attacks, in some cases surpassing the attacks reported by honeypot sensors located in developed countries. We therefore show that networks in Africa are as vulnerable, exposed, and at risk as networks in other continents. Our analysis also shows that some attacks are directed to specific continents or networks across the world.

In the remainder of the paper, we present an overview of honeypot systems in Section 2. In Section 3, we present deployment requirements for SGNET. In Section 4 we analyze the collected data and discuss on our findings. In Section 5 we discuss a summarised analysis of results from nodes in Africa and finally conclude the paper in Section 6.

2   A Review of Honeypot Systems

We have presented a definition of honeypot sensor from [3] as a security resource whose value lies in being probed, attacked, or compromised. There are however varying other definitions of honeypot, leading to some miscommunication and confusion amongst researchers. Some researchers refer to honeypot as an intrusion detection tool, whereas others think it is a deception tool. There are those who think it is a weapon to lure hackers, and still others believe a honeypot should emulate vulnerabilities, and some view honeypots as controlled production systems that attackers can break into.

One of the well-known research initiative on honeypot technologies was called *honeynet* project [5]. A *honeynet* is a type of honeypot designed primarily to gather information on the enemy for research purposes. The honeynet project began in 1999 for the purpose of gathering intelligence on attacker techniques, tools and motives that might help the security community identify new threats and weaknesses more effectively.

Honeypots are classified according to their level of interaction with the attacker. There are *low-interaction, mid-interaction, high-interaction* honeypots [6]. Low-interaction honeypots expose to attackers certain *fake* (emulated) services which are implemented by listening on specific port (services are limited to specific listening ports). With low-interaction honeypot, there is no real operating system target that an attacker can operate on. An example of low-interaction honeypot is *honeyd*, which is an open source designed to run primarily on Unix systems [7].

Mid-interaction honeypots provide more sophisticated *fake daemons* with deeper knowledge about the specific services they provide. With this, the attacker is able to detect a real operating system and has more possibilities to interact and probe the system. The daemons involved need to be as secure as possible. Examples of mid-interaction honeypots are *honeyd and Specter*. Finally, high-interaction honeypots involve a real operating system that is offered to the attacker, thus providing the attacker with capabilities to upload and install new services or applications. All actions are monitored and recorded in order to gather more information about the blackhat community. This means that the system must be under monitoring all the time.

Distributed honeypot systems are built using a number of connected honeypot sensors that are configured across the Internet. They therefore provide platforms to compare attacks experienced at different locations, and to study propagation of existing and newly emerging attacks.

There are a number of projects based on distributed honeypot platforms. For example, a research project called Collection and Analysis of Data from Honeypots (CADHo project) [10], DShield Project [12], MyNetWatchman [13], and Internet Telescope project CAIDA [14].

As earlier mentioned, the most recent distributed honeypot platform is SGNET [4]. SGNET is a low-interaction honeypot system that exploits the strengths of ScriptGen technology and dynamically combines with other existing solutions namely Argos and Nepenthes. ScriptGen is an automated script generation tool for honeyd, Nepenthes is a honeypot with specific objective to download malware from attacking sources, and Argos is an emulator for Fingerprinting Zero-Day Attacks. SGNET is capable of offering an overlay based on an ad-hoc HTTP-like protocol called Peiros to coordinate its entities and integrate them into a distributed architecture. The ultimate result of this integration is a distributed honeypot deployment that automatically learns and handles server-based exploits, and emulates the code injection attacks up to the point of the malware download.

SGNET has been used by researchers to study various behaviors and attributes of Internet attacks and their underlying attack tools [6, 8, 9]. In this paper, we use SGNET to particularly compare Internet attacks between honeypot sensors in Africa with sensors located in other continents.

3   Deployment of Honeypot Sensor Using SGNET

To be able to collect attack data and have access to data from other honeypot sensors across the world, we deployed honeypot sensor in our local network in Uganda and connected it to the SGNET platform. The process of deploying a honeypot sensor is fully automated. Interested parties in participating in the Leurrecom.org project provide a dedicated computing and networking environment with minimal stipulated requirements whereas the institute that oversees the honeypot project provides an installation CD, access to the collected data and analysis tools as well as integrity of data collected.

SGNET based deployment uses a collection of several tools and functional modules to build what we call a distributed honeypot system. Such tools are Argos, Nepenthese, VirusTotal, Anubis, Maxmind, and P0fv2. The data collected from all sensors in the network is automatically uploaded into a central database on daily basis. Different datasets that are collected from all the participating partners is accessible through a Web interface to all participating partners for easy analysis of the data.

4   Comparative Analysis of Attacks

In this section we discuss the findings we derived from analyzing the collected data. Specifically, we compare and analyze the attacks experienced by honeypot sensors on per continent basis. We use the data collected during six months period starting from Dec 2009 to May 2010 to compare how vulnerable are honeypot sensors (also networks) in Africa compared to honeypot sensors located in other continents. During the six months, a total of 33 honeypot sensors were active in five continents, namely Europe, North America, Asia, Australia, and Africa.

Figure 1 shows the number of active honeypot sensors by continent. We can see that Europe had by far the largest number of sensors; 23 active sensors which make about 70% of the total active sensors. This shows the involvement of European research community in network security issues. Perhaps it also shows how cautious the Europeans are on network security. The figure shows that North America had four active honeypot sensors while the rest of the continents had two active sensors each. The active nodes in Africa were located in Uganda and Egypt. Interestingly, during the whole six months of our project running, we have

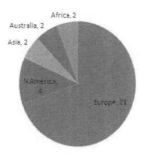

Fig. 1. Number of Active Honeypot Sensors per Continent

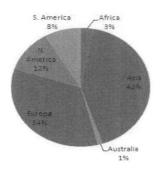

Fig. 2. Attack sources per continent

not observed any active sensor in South America. It was however also observed that there were honeypot sensors in the network that were part of the distributed honeypot system but were not active during the time when measurements were collected.

In the following sections, we present an indepth comparative analysis of specific attacks sources and actual attacks that were experienced by sensor nodes in each continent.

4.1   Analysis of Attack Sources

In this section we compare the sources of attacks originating from each continent. An attack source is identified by an IP address from which the attack is originated. We first look at the distribution of attack sources by continent and then investigate the countries that generate significant sources of attacks towards each continent.

In total, an overwhelming 1,042,282 attack sources have been recorded during a period of six months. Figure 2 shows the percentage of attack sources per continent. We can see from the figure that Asia generated 42% of all attacks which amounts to 438,209 attack sources. Europe is also reported to have contributed to a large fraction of attack sources of 34%. This is a total of 354,056 attack sources originating from Europe. Attack sources from North America made 12% of total number of attack sources, which is equivalent to 120,455 attack sources. South America generated 88,236 attack sources, Africa 29,946 attack sources, and Australia 11,380 attack sources which contributed to 8%, 3% and 1% of the total attack sources respectively. Africa and Australia have the least number of attack sources as compared to the rest of the continents.

It is perhaps a fact that, the more Internet users in a continent, the more malicious users are likely to be as well. That is why we have fewer attacks from Africa and Australia compared to attacks from Europe, Asia, North America and South America. It is however interesting to observe that Africa generates a sizeable number of attacks which is more than in Australia. Detailed analysis of the data is not shown in Figure 2. Most of the attacks from Africa are observed to originate from Gabon and South Africa.

Table 1. Score of attack sources by country of origin

Origin	EU1	EU2	AS1	AS2	NA1	NA2	AU1	AU2	AF1	AF2
Russia	10	10	10	1	7	8	5	7	6	6
USA	9	9	9	3	10	9	9	9	8	9
China	8	8	8	9	9	10	10	10	9	10
Taiwan	7	5	6	7	4	5	4	5	-	7
Italy	6	6	5	-	-	4	-	-	-	-
Denmark	4	4	3	-	-	1	-	-	-	-
Romania	5	2	4	-	-	-	-	-	-	-
Brazil	-	7	7	4	5	6 -	6	6	-	4
Peru	-	3	-	6	-	-	-	-	-	-
Japan	3	-	2	8	3	-	3	4	-	-
Poland	2	-	-	-	-	-	-	-	-	-
T. Tobago	-	1	-	5	-	-	-	-	4	8
Argentina	1	-	-	-	-	-	-	-	-	-
Colombia	-	-	-	2	-	-	-	-	-	-
Gabon	-	-	-	-	1	-	1	1	3	-
Pakistan	-	-	-	-	2	-	-	-	-	-
France	-	-	-	-	-	-	-	2	5	2
Estonia	-	-	-	-	-	3	-	-	7	-
Portugal	-	-	-	-	-	-	-	-	2	1
India	-	-	-	10	-	-	-	-	-	-
Canada	-	-	-	-	6	2	2	3	-	3
Australia	-	-	-	-	-	-	7	-	-	-
Latvia	-	-	-	-	-	-	-	-	10	-

We further selected two most attacked sensors from each of the five continents and analyzed the recorded attack sources by each sensor. We denote EU1 and EU2 the two sensors located in Europe, AS1 and AS2 are located in Asia, NA1 and NA2 are located in North America, AF1 and AF2 are located in Africa and

AU1 and AU2 are located in Australia. For each honeypot sensor, we identified top 10 countries with the most attack sources that were recorded by each identified sensor. We then gave scores to each country such that the country with most attack sources is given the highest score of 10 and the one with least sources is scored 1. This enables us to compare the sources of attacks in terms of specific countries that attacked different continents. We present the results in Table 1.

We can observe a few patterns from the table. Firstly, the three countries with most attack sources (Russia, China, USA) seem to attack all continents almost equally, i.e., their scores in each continent don't vary too much. This shows that either there are many attack sources in these countries, and/or the sources indiscriminately broadcast their attacks on the Internet, i.e, without specific target in mind. In contrast, the table also shows that sources from some countries tend to target networks in specific countries. For instance, India has a score of 10 and appears only in Asia which means there are many attackers in India that target networks only in Asia. Similar pattern is observed for the case of Pakistan and Canada. We also observe that most attacks recorded by one honeypot node in Africa were from Latvia (score 10) and Estonia (score 7), which are not the most attacking countries to other continents. Trinidad and Tobago also oddly appears to strongly attack the other sensor in Africa. Also interesting to note is Portugal appearing only on the top 10 list of African honeypots. Other similarly odd observations are seen for Argentina, Trinidad and Tobago, Colombia, and France. These attacks may be due to compromised machines in those countries.

The results in Table 1 reveal that while majority of the attacks originate from specific countries that indiscriminately attack networks, some attacks seem to be targeting specific networks. In particular, we observe that African nodes are vulnerable to attacks that originate from isolated countries. This is a clear evidence of directed attacks to specific networks.

In the following section, we analyze in details the specific attacks registered by most honeypot sensors. Some of these attacks include code injection attacks, malware download, backscatter attacks and targeted ports.

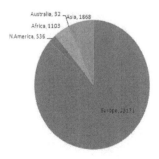

Fig. 3. Code Injection Attack Sources by Continent

Code injection attack sources. Code injection is the exploitation of a computing system bug that is caused by processing invalid data. It can be used by an attacker to introduce (or "inject") code into a computer program to change the course of execution. The results of a code injection attack can be disastrous. In a period of six months, a total of 26,710 code injection attack sources was observed by all honeypot sensors. Europe recorded the largest percentage of code injection attacks with 23,171 code injection attack sources as seen from Figure 3. Asia follows in the second position with 1,868 attack sources.

It is perhaps surprising that honeypot sensors in Africa reported more code injection attack sources compared to sensors in continents such as North America where we expect more attacks because of more Internet activities. These results further asserts our previous observation that having less Internet activities does not guarantee security against Internet threats, and it is highly likely that some attackers tend to target locations where Internet penetration is low assuming that security awareness level in those countries is low.

Backscatter attack sources. Backscatter attacks occur when a flood of messages is received with a forged sender address as spam messages. A total of 25 Backscatter attacks sources were observed targeting those sensors. These attacks were recorded on only three honeypot sensors; two located in Europe and one located in Australia.

Analysis of targeted ports/port sequences. Attacks tend to attack different ports based on a certain sequence while others target individual ports directly. The sequence of ports attacked is also an inherent feature for some attack tools. Analysis of attack ports sequences is used to understand the nature of the attacker. Table 2 shows the distribution of sources received by each port or port sequence per continent.

Table 2. Attacked Ports

Port Sequence	Europe	Asia	Africa	N. America	Australia
445	380,233	70,450	54,783	1,460	347
135	836,099	3,321	3,367	1,141	203
23	35,048	3,280	544	329	436
44-139	120,039	21,458	2,740	904	112
445-80	95,920	20,411	2,028	31	2
445-139-80	22,815	16,873	1,707	31	14
80-445	10,842	2,423	147	0	0
80-445-139	12,625	2,349	141	0	0

Attack process against these ports seems to be fairly regular. We also observe that most sources have sent their requests to port 445 (Microsoft-ds). Comparing to other continents, Europe recorded a much larger number of attacks at port 135 (Microsoft RPC), which is similar to port sequence 44-139. We again see from the table that honeypot sensors in Africa experienced more cases of targeted ports than other continents notably North America and Australia. In some cases, for instance, port 445 attacks, the difference is significantly large.

5 Analysis of Attacks for African Nodes

In summary, we have observed that Africa honeypot sensors have been subjected to similar attacks with other honeypots located in different continents. Some of these attacks include code injection attacks, backscatter attacks, malware downloaded and specific ports being targeted by the attacks. In this section, we look at attacks for African honeypot nodes.

African sensors recorded a total of 29,946 attack sources and of these attack sources, 1,103 were code injection attacks, with Egypt sensor registering most attacks equal to 596 attack sources and Ugandan sensor experienced 507 code injection attack sources. From Table 1, we see that the two sensors in Africa are attacked by sources China, USA, and Russia at almost equal intensity. However, the sensor in Egypt was uniquely attacked by sources from Taiwan, Brazil, and Canada whereas the sensor in Uganda was uniquely attacked by sources from Latvia and Estonia.

We also observed that the honeypot sensor in Egypt experienced more attacks on targeted ports than the sensor in Uganda. However, the pattern isn't uniform when one looks at individual ports. For instance, the sensor in Uganda experienced more attacks on ports 135 and 23 recording 2,411, and 501 compared to 926 and 43 for Egypt respectively. It is difficult to know why there was more interest to attack some specific ports on the network in Uganda than on the network in Egypt.

6 Conclusion

In this paper, we deployed a honeypot sensor in a local network in Uganda and connected it to a distributed honeypot sensor system called SGNET. We collected data from the local sensor and all other active sensors in the distributed honeypot system to study and compare the attacks reported.

We observed from our analysis of the data that networks in Africa experience a significant amount of attacks in some cases surpassing the attacks experienced by networks in developed continents such as North America and Australia. We also discovered that some attacks sources constantly target specific networks such as networks in Africa and Asia. In summary, the Internet doesn't have any boarders to block against attacks. This demands for a special care to be taken when deploying networks anywhere in the world. There is a need to setup honeypot sensors in different locations in the world in order to collect data that will provide a complete picture and wider comparison of Internet attacks and their behaviors.

Acknowledgement. This work was partially supported by the Cisco University Research Fund, a corporate adviced fund of Silicom Valley Community Foundation.

References

1. Team Cymru, The darknet project, http://www.cymru.com/darknet/ (accessed 04/03/2010)
2. Internet Motion Sensor, http://ims.eecs.umich.edu/ (accessed 01/03/2010)
3. Spitzner, L.: Honeypots, Tracking Hackers. Addison Wesley, Boston (2002)
4. Leita, C., Pham, V.H., Thonnard, O., Ramirez-Silva, E., Pouget, F., Kirda, E., Dacier, M.: The Leurrecom.org Project, Collecting Internet threats information using a worldwide distributed honeynet (June 2008)
5. Spitzner, L.: Know your enemy, Honeynets. In: AusCERT 2004 Conference, Technical Stream (2004)
6. Pouget, F., Dacier, M., Debar, H.: Honeypot, Honeynet, Honetoken Terminological issues. Technical report, Institute Eurecom and France Telecom RD, France (2003)
7. Provos, N.: Honeyd, A virtual Honeypot Daemon, Center for Information Technology Integration, University of Michigan (2002)
8. Kaaniche, M., Alata, E., Nicomette, V., Deswarte, Y., Dacier, M.: Empirical analysis and statistical modeling of attack processes based on honeypots. Conjuction with the International Conference of Dependable Systems and Networks (June 2006)
9. Pouget, F., Dacier, M., Pham, V.H.: On the advantages of deploying a large scale distributed honeypot platform on the Internet. In: First Workshop on Quality of Protection (2005)
10. Alata, E., Dacier, M.: Collection and analysis of attack data based on honeypots deployed on the Internet. In: First Workshop on Quality of protection (2004)
11. Pouget, F., Dacier, M., Chen, P.T., Laih, C.S.: Comparative survey of local honeypot sensors to assist network forensics. In: SADFE 2005, 1st International Workshop on Systematic Approaches to Digital Forensic Engineering, Institut Eurcom and National Cheng Kung University (2005)
12. Hofman, M.: DShield distributed intrusion detection system, http://www.dshield.org (accessed May 23, 2010)
13. Baldwin, L.: myNetWatchman, Network intrusion detection and reporting, http://www.mynetwatchman.com (accessed December 29, 2009)
14. Shannon, C., Moore, D.: CAIDA Project, The UCSD Network Telescope, The spread of the witty worm, www.caida.org/publications/papers/2004/witty (accessed April 15, 2010)
15. Leita, C., Dacier, M.: SGNET, A worldwide, deployment framework to support the analysis of malware threat models. In: Proceedings of the 7th European Dependable Computing Conference (2008)

Detecting Network Intrusions Using Hierarchical Temporal Memory

Gift Khangamwa

Lecturer, Computing & Information Technology Department,
University of Malawi, The Polytechnic
giftkhangamwa@yahoo.com, gkhangamwa@poly.ac.mw

Abstract. Intrusion Detection Systems (IDS) are a very popular network security tool. These tools can allow network administrators, to identify and react to hostile traffic aimed at, or generated from their own network. In general there are two common Intrusion Detection approaches which are behavior or traffic anomaly based and knowledge or signature based. As a result of the increased sophistication of intrusion attacks, one very desirable feature of advanced IDS is to be capable of learning and generalizing from known traffic patterns of a system, process or a user's behavior. In this project we investigated the use of a novel Artificial Intelligence (AI) approach to intrusion detection based on network traffic anomaly detection. The AI technique used is based on the Hierarchical Temporal Memory (HTM) paradigm developed by Numenta, which is a relatively new AI concept that mimics the operation of the neocortex area of the human brain[11,14]. The developed AI scheme was evaluated using the corpus of data from Massachusetts Institute of Technology, Lincoln Laboratories in USA [20]. Our results show that HTM based intrusion detection can achieve relatively high success rates in identifying anomalous traffic in computer networks, furthermore our research also shows that HTM based schemes can achieve very fast detection rates making them a very good alternative for real time intrusion detection engine.

In this paper we present the results of our study as well as a discussion on our future work.

Keywords: Intrusion detection, Artificial Intelligence, Hierarchical Temporal Memory[TM], Network anomaly detection.

1 Introduction

The research presented in this paper is motivated by the need for intrusion detection mechanisms that are capable of dealing with the increasing security challenges faced by modern computer and data networks. Authors in [10] speak of the challenges that computers that are hooked to the internet face due to the security challenges in open environments like the internet. This has made intrusion detection systems an absolute necessity in this information age, more so in the developing world where ICT infrastructure developments are still in early stages. This means that as dependence on the internet grows so will the prevalence of intrusions and hence also the importance of intrusion detection systems to deter such attacks.

R. Popescu-Zeletin et al. (Eds.): AFRICOMM 2010, LNICST 64, pp. 41–48, 2011.
© Institute for Computer Sciences, Social Informatics and Telecommunications Engineering 2011

According to [10], the sophistication of attacks and tools used by attackers has been steadily advancing. This implies that new attacks are ever being devised and even old attacks are being modified to be made stealthier, and more undetectable.

The aim of this research was to investigate the usage of NuPIC (Hierarchical Temporal Memory technology) from Numenta Inc. for use in Network Intrusion detection. NuPIC is an artificial intelligence based platform that is built from a theory of the neocortex of the human brain. The platform used for this research was obtained freely under a research license. This technology has the capacity to detect both modified attack signatures as well as novel attacks, because it uses machine learning to learn and generalize from attack patterns that it is trained with. Consequently such a scheme will help to ensure that any known or unknown attacks are identified and reported.

The scheme was tested using the Massachusetts Institute of Technology Lincoln laboratories, 1999 DARPA Intrusion Detection Systems data corpora. This data is freely available online from www.ll.mit.edu and contains labeled anomalies; this data has also been used by authors in [1, 8 and 9].

2 Literature Review

Intrusion detection and Intrusion Detection systems have been defined in so many different ways by different authors in the literature. Some of the definitions that capture the important principles involved are as follows: Systems aimed at detecting attacks against computer systems and networks [5]. In his book on Intrusion Detection, Amoroso in [7] defined it as a process of identifying and responding to malicious activity targeted at computing and networking resources. Bace in [6] stated it as, a system that monitors computer networks and systems for violations of security policy. While Mukherjee et al, in [1] stated that, it's an approach of providing a sense of security in existing computers and data networks while allowing them to operate in their open Environment where threats are ever present. All these definitions capture the major aspects and principles of this discipline and provide an understanding of what IDS are; our work in this research is hence built upon this understanding. Authors in [1] used a technique based on neural networks, which also have the capacity for machine learning. The major weakness for neural networks is that it is not possible to analyze how the neural network learned and come to the conclusions that it makes and uses to make detections [3]. The major difference between their method and the strategy used in this study is the technology used, at the time of conducting this research there was no available literature on usage of this technology for Intrusion detection. HTM technology offers a better alternative to neural networks because once the network has been trained it can be analysed to access how the learning was done. Furthermore network training using HTMs is transparent and controllable through some parameters that can be changed. The authors in [3] also used neural networks for intrusion detection. The only difference in their method from that used in [1] is that they used misuse detection where detection is based on training a detection system using a known set of anomalies and the system then uses this knowledge to make detections, while the other authors in[1] used both anomaly and misuse detection using neural networks for intrusion detection.

2.1 Intrusion Detection

In this research our focus is mainly on approach to intrusion detection that falls under the classification that is based on detection method. We consider Intrusion Detection based on what data is used to establish a baseline for detection of anomalous or intrusive situations. Here two primary methods are identified:

2.1.1 Misuse Detection
Misuse detection [1, 2, 3, 6, 8, 9] or otherwise referred to as, signature based by [8, 9] or Knowledge based [5]. In this approach an Intrusion detection system is trained with patterns or signatures of all known anomalies. This implies that the system will have complete knowledge of all the anomalies for whose signatures or patterns it is equipped with. Therefore using this information, the system is able to identify these patterns and signatures in any current or ongoing network traffic [4].

2.1.1.1 Benefits. This approach has the benefit that it identifies the known anomalies with very high accurate rates, while at the same time yielding very low false positive rates [1].

2.1.1.2 Weaknesses. The major weaknesses of this approach are that it cannot identify novel (never seen before) attacks [1, 2, 8, and 9]; it also cannot identify known anomalies that leave different attack signatures in a system after every attack [1]. Hence even known attacks that evolve will not be identified by this methodology.

2.1.2 Anomaly Detection
Anomaly Detection [1, 2, 3, 8, 9] otherwise also referred to as Behavior Based [5] which models the normal anomaly free state of a network or system [7, 8, 18]. So in this scheme the system will mistrust any other pattern that deviates from what it knows as the normal state of the network or system.

2.1.2.1 Benefits. This scheme has the obvious benefit that anomalies that have never been seen before can be identified and detected [8, 9].

The AI method used in this study is suitable for both misuse detection based as well as anomaly detection based approaches to intrusion detection. Similar work was done by Ghosh and Schwartzbard in [1] where they used Artificial Neural Networks for both misuse and anomaly detection. Though we will discuss misuse detection in this paper our major focus in will be on anomaly detection.

2.1.2.2 Weaknesses. The problem with anomaly detection is that it is likely to raise many false alarms [2]. This is more true if the method used is incapable of recognizing novel legitimate behavior of the system as is the case where non machine learning approaches are used.

2.2 Hierarchical Temporal Memory

Numenta Platform for Intelligent Computing models the functioning of the neocortex of the human brain, without being a direct implementation of the same. This makes it potentially able to solve different kinds of problems that are easy for humans to solve but are extremely hard for computers to solve.

HTM uses a hierarchy of learning nodes that are capable of identifying spatial and temporal correlations to formulate a collection of beliefs of the existing causes in their world, as presented in the input data. According to [14], HTMs are organized as a tree-shaped hierarchy of nodes, where each learning node implements a common learning and memory function. HTMs store information throughout the hierarchy in a way that models the world. All objects in the world, be they cars, people, buildings, speech, or the flow of information across a computer network, have structure. This structure is hierarchical in both space and time. HTM memory is also hierarchical in both space and time, and therefore can efficiently capture and model the structure of the world.

Every node in an HTM network has 2 components a Spatial Pooler component and a Temporal Pooler component. On any given input the Spatial Pooler reduces a huge number of input occurrences to a smaller set of values called coincidences. These coincidences are fed to a Temporal Pooler which classifies them into groups basing on their similarities i.e. spatial and temporal correlations.

The HTM network therefore learns via belief propagation of knowledge from lower level nodes to nodes higher up in the hierarchy. This means what the HTM network knows finally is a summary of what all the nodes at different levels in the hierarchy have learnt during training.

At the time of the study the version of nupic used was 1.6.1 which was the latest at the time.

3 Experimental Setup

The experimental setup in this research involved setting up and configuring NuPIC platform and building NuPIC HTM networks in a computer lab. The HTM networks were then tested using corpora of data that was assembled by the Massachusetts Institute of Technology, Lincoln Laboratories as part of the 1999 DARPA Intrusion Detection Systems Evaluation project. According to authors in [20], the aim of the project was to produce corpora of data that were extensive covering a wide range of intrusions and making the data readily accessible to researchers and developers, to be used in the evaluation of intrusion detection systems worldwide.

In this research the tests were designed to assess if the NuPIC platform was suitable for the general problem of intrusion detection and more specifically anomaly detection. Furthermore more tests were conducted in order to ascertain other factors that might affect the performance of the developed HTM network based intrusion detection scheme under investigation.

4 Results

The experimental setup in this research involved setting up and configuring NuPIC platform and building NuPIC HTM networks in a computer lab. The HTM networks built were used to answer a number questions like is this technology appropriate for intrusion detection. Secondly how can detection of intrusions be improved when this scheme is being used. Below is a presentation of the results that were obtained during the experiments.

4.1 Proof of Concept

In this test the objective was to test and find out if indeed using the NuPIC platform we could detect the presence of anomalies in the data. In order to do this a 3 layer network with 14 learning nodes was built and tested with 64 x 400 training data, the results obtained are:

- **88.25** % Accuracy on Training data
- **88.25** % Accuracy on Testing data

Accuracy is defined as the percentage of correctly matching the actual categories of anomalies learnt or discovered by the NuPIC network against the actual categories of anomalies passed to it in a category file. This is hence a good measure of how well a NuPIC network performs.

4.2 Factors Affecting Performance

In these set of tests different HTM networks were built in-order to discover the factors that affect their performance.

4.2.1 Varying Number of Anomalies in Training Data

In this test case, the number of anomalies in the training data is varied incrementally from 1 up to 4 different types of anomalies. This is done for scenarios where specific anomalies are used and also where categories of anomalies are used. The table below outlines some of the anomalies that were used both for the specific anomaly scenario and also for the categorized anomaly scenario. Below are the names of some of the anomalies used in the study;

Table 1. Specific and Categorized anomalies

Specific Anomalies	Categorized Anomalies
HTTPTUNNEL, PORTSCAN, XLOCK, XTERM, SECRET	DOS, PROBE, U2R , R2L , DATA

The graphs below show the outcome of plotting the percent accuracy of training and detection against different numbers of anomalies in the training data.

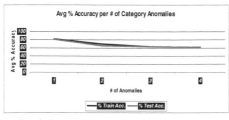

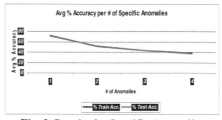

Fig. 1. Results for Categorized Anomalies   **Fig. 2.** Results for Specific Anomalies

The 2 lines in the graphs above refer to the percent accuracy obtained during training of the network (% train acc.) and the other line refers to the accuracy obtained with novel (unseen before) data during detection (% test acc.).

4.2.2 Varying Number of Learning Nodes in the HTM Network

In this test case the number of learning nodes per level in the HTM networks used as well as the number of levels of nodes was varied. Two general network designs were used in this case. The first design is a 3 layer network having 8 learning nodes at the first level, 4 learning nodes at the second level and 2 learning nodes at the third level. The second design is a 2 layer network having 4 learning nodes at the first level and 2 learning nodes at the second level. In all these designs the other factor that was also varied was the number of vectors or rows of values in each training file. HTM learning nodes accept integer vectors that it uses to build a model of its world [16]. Having done this each Network design was subjected to tests using a 32 vector input file as well as a 64 vector input file. This means the 32 vector training file had 32 columns while the 64 vector training file had 64 columns; the number of rows was kept constant per test.

Table 2. Test results for HTM networks

Anomaly	Test	set 1	set 2	anomaly	test	set 1	set 2
Secret	1	75.76142	72.26463	Secret	3	81.25	81.17048
Portsweep	1	75.892857	76.41026	portsweep	3	79.75	77.94872
Xlock	1	63.3587766	63.93862	Xlock	3	63.5	63.93862
Xterm	1	72.900763	74.93606	Xterm	3	81	78.77238
Mailbomb	1	73.7913486	73.91304	Mailbomb	3	75.5	75.19182
Httptunnel	1	68.298969	68.65285	Httptunnel	3	91.5	90.15544
Secret	2	76.14213	76.33588	Secret	4	80.75	79.13486
Portsweep	2	79.846939	80.51282	Portsweep	4	83.23	81.79487
Xlock	2	53.94402	54.4757	Xlock	4	68.25	68.28645
Xterm	2	62.595419	74.68031	Xterm	4	76.5	74.68031
Mailbomb	2	72.0101781	72.37852	Mailbomb	4	73	73.14578
Httptunnel	2	80.670103	82.38342	Httptunnel	4	88.75	87.56477

4.2.3 Measuring Time to Detect Anomaly in Test Data

The results presented here are for a series of tests to measure the amount of time taken to detect anomalies, using two network types as in the test above;

Table 3. Time Taken to Detect Anomaly

	2 Layer Network	3 Layer Network
# of Anomalies	Detection time (sec)	Detection time (sec)
1	0.85949996	1.023499932
2	1.7030002	2.358000135
3	2.24249998	3.625000057
4	3.18699984	2.898499315
Average	1.997999995	2.47624986

5 Conclusions

The conclusions arrived at in this study, after looking at all the experiments that were run and also, considering the results that were obtained are as follows:

NuPIC platform is suitable for solving the problem of Intrusion Detection; using either anomaly detection based approach or even misuse detection based approach can be accommodated. Nevertheless this method is most suitable for anomaly detection as it tends to perform best with a single anomaly training data scenario. This means that it is much easier to build an HTM based anomaly detection system that will be trained with a single data and be capable of making detections of any deviations from normal behavior as well as any modifications of some known anomalies. Furthermore the HTM networks tend to perform better if they are given the data representing a global view of a computer network.

Secondly the results indicated that training a network with a single pattern led to more effective HTM networks. This means that HTMs are more suitable for anomaly detection based systems as opposed to misuse detection. The HTM network can be trained with normal state data and be used to detect any deviation from this norm as an anomaly.

Thirdly the design of a NuPIC network is very important as it affects how best a network will be trained and hence also its ability to make predictions and inferences. In addition to this, the input training file needs to have more vectors to ensure that each learning node receives sufficient data for it to learn the patterns in data easily and pass its belief distribution to the nodes above it.

Finally the trained NuPIC networks were capable of making detections in less than 3 seconds. This implies that HTM based IDS can be used for real-time detections. This is very important for real-time online IDS since some attacks are rather short and require very fast anomaly detection in order to secure data and other computing resources.

References

1. Ghosh, A.K., Schwartzbard, A.: A Study in Using Neural Networks for Anomaly and Misuse Detection. In: Proceedings of the 3rd USENIX Windows NT Symposium, Seattle, Washington, July 12-15 (1999)
2. Ryan, J., Lin, M.-J., Miikkulainen, R.: Intrusion Detection with Neural Networks. AAAI Technical Report, Vol. WS-97-07, pp. 72–77 (1997)
3. Cannady, J.: Artificial Neural Networks for Misuse Detection. In: Proceedings of the 1998 National Information Systems Security Conference (NISSC 1998), October 5-8, pp. 443–456 (1998)
4. Helmer, G.G., Wong, J.S.K., Honavar, V., Miller, L.: Intelligent Agents for Intrusion Detection, Iowa State University
5. Debar, H., Dacier, M., Wespi, A.: Towards a Taxonomy of Intrusion Detection Systems. Computer Networks 31, 805–822 (1999)
6. Bace, R.G.: Intrusion Detection. Macmillan Technical Publishing, Indianapolis (2000)
7. Amoroso, E.G.: Intrusion Detection: An Introduction to Internet Surveillance, Correlation, Traps, Trace Back, and Response. AT&T Laboratories (1999)

8. Paschalidis, I.C., Smaragdakis, G.: Spatio-Temporal Network Anomaly Detection by Assessing Deviations of Empirical Measures
9. Paschalidis, I.C., Smaragdakis, G.: A large Deviations Approach to Statistical Traffic Anomaly Detection
10. Allen, J., Christie, A., Fithen, W., McHugh, J., Pickel, J., Stoner, E.: State of the Practice of Intrusion Detection Technologies, Carnegie Mellon, Software Engineering Institute, Technical Report CMU/SEI-99-TR-028, Networked Systems Survivability Program (January 2000)
11. Numenta Inc., Getting Started with NuPIC, Document Version 1.2.1 (2008)
12. Numenta Inc., Advanced NuPIC programming, Document Version 1.8.1 (2008)
13. George, D., Jaros, B.: Numenta Inc., The HTM Learning Algorithms (2007)
14. Hawkins, J., George, D.: Numenta Inc., Hierachical Temporal Memory: Concepts, Theory and Terminology (2006)
15. Numenta Inc., Hierarchical Temporal Memory: Comparison with Existing Models, version 1.01 (2007)
16. Numenta Inc., Problems that Fit HTM, version 1.0 (2007)
17. Koutsoutos, S., Christou, I.T., Efremidis, S.: A Classifier Ensemble Approach to Intrusion Detection for Network Initiated Attacks. In: Emerging Artificial Intelligence Applications in Computer Engineering. IOS Press, Amsterdam (2007)
18. Mukherjee, B., Heberlein, L.T., Levitt, K.N.: Network Intrusion Detection. IEEE Network (1994)
19. Lee, W., Stolfo, S.J., Chan, P.K., Eskin, E., Fan, W., Miller, M., Hershkop, S., Zhang, J.: Real Time Data Mining-based Intrusion Detection
20. Haines, J.W., Lippmann, R.P., Fried, D.J., Zissman, M.A., Tran, E., Boswell, S.B.: DARPA Intrusion Detection and Procedures, February 2001, Technical Report 1062 (1999)

Global Survey on Culture Differences and Context in Using E-Government Systems: A Pilot Study

Marlien Herselman and Darelle van Greunen

Nelson Mandela Metropolitan University
Port Elizabeth, South Africa
mherselman@csir.co.za, Darelle.vanGreunen@nmmu.ac.za

Abstract. The purpose of this paper is to discuss some preliminary results, which were collected from a global survey on cultural differences and context in using e-government website services. The primary objective of this research is to make suggestions that could contribute to a more effective and usable e-Government website in the specific countries taking into account the cultural context of the society it is serving. This s important and can be used to assist governments to ensure their website address the needs of specific contexts of their users. The focus of this research will be on the selected populations with the emphasis on culture context as a cultural dimension. In order to measure the cultural profile of the selected populations, a questionnaire was applied. Ten participants were identified through purposive sampling and divided into two groups (5) in low-context culture and (5) in high-context culture. Six tables represent three different sections for both groups. The three sections are preferences general websites, preferences in government web sites and culture characteristics in society. The results contradicted the literature in three tables and the most significant results are that high-context participants changed their preferences when using government websites although they preferred high-context styles for general Internet usage which was not the case for government websites. Here they preferred more low-context styles. Another result was that high-context participants had characteristics of which were more representative of low-context cultures and vice versa.

Keywords: global study, culture context, culture, e-government.

1 Introduction

This paper will mainly focus on results from a pilot study which was done on a global scale to determine the influence of culture and context on e-government services. Design in the context of the Web is not only about visual things – aesthetics, layout, colour – but about a dynamic interaction between users (citizens) and an organization (government) providing a service. Therefore it is important to understand the interaction-based design and factors related to e-government and how different cultures all over the world engage with these or what their perceptions are about this service. Its relevance to the scientific community is therefore also important as developers of websites need to be aware of these preferences of different types of users in their specific contexts.

R. Popescu-Zeletin et al. (Eds.): AFRICOMM 2010, LNICST 64, pp. 49–68, 2011.
© Institute for Computer Sciences, Social Informatics and Telecommunications Engineering 2011

Citizens want more than privacy and security protection they want the same efficiency, convenience and service orientation that they experienced in their dealings with private sector companies.

Difference in culture, as was found by Hofstede [1] shows there are significant differences between nations, which can lead to differences between national groups within the same organization. Hofstede [1] specifically indicates that there are five cultural dimensions which are power distance index (PDI) which indicates that power is distributed unequally, individualism (IDV) where everyone looks after themselves and their immediate families, masculinity (MAS) where the focus is the role distribution between males and females, uncertainty avoidance index (UAI) which shows how comfortable or uncomfortable members are with unstructured situations and finally long-term orientation (LTO) which focus on how people achieve their goals in society.

According to a few authors [2], [3] and [4] culture focuses on three concepts: context, time and space. These views on culture can have the effect that those groups can either understand knowledge differently or have significant barriers to participating in the sharing of knowledge. Culture is so embedded into people's lives that our ignorance of it usually leads to failures. Therefore systems designers within organizations should have as much knowledge as possible about culture to escape mistakes made due to a lack of cultural awareness and understanding.

This can be regarded as a pilot study of the global survey. The survey is in the form of an online questionnaire. It examines user preferences and perceptions in terms of the culture-context dimension. The dimension itself is analysed in terms of web site design and cultural characteristics within a society. This is a qualitative research study to elicit the experiences of different types of users in different types of context as to their preferences of using e-government websites. Purposive sampling was applied to select a representative sample.

A background discussion regarding the culture-context dimension and its role within society and web design will be conducted. Following this will be a brief discussion on how the preliminary results will be analysed.

2 Background Information

The background discussion on the culture-context dimension will be based on three perspectives:

- Definition
- Country classification
- Web design features.

2.1 Definition

"A high-context (HC) communication or message is one in which most of the information is already in the person, while very little is in the coded, explicitly transmitted part of the message. A low-context (LC) communication is just the opposite; i.e., the mass of the information is vested in the explicit code" [5].

Depending on whether meaning comes from the setting or from the words that are being exchanged in a communication, cultures can be categorised as either being a high- or low-context society [6]. There is a dramatic distinction between cultures as to how much of the context or environment is important and meaningful within a communication event.

In a low-context culture, the surrounding context has no influence on the communication event. It is the message itself that provides all the meaning. In a high-context society, cultures will assign great value and meaning too many of the stimuli that surround an explicit message [7] so verbal messages on their own have very little meaning: it is the surrounding context that will provide meaning to the verbal messages.

2.2 Country Classification

There is a general idea as to which countries are classified as high-context cultures and which are classified as low-context cultures. Low-context countries primarily consist of countries from North America and much of Western Europe. High-context cultures primarily consist of countries from Asia, Africa, South America and much of the Middle East [8; 9].

Figure 1 displays the hierarchy of countries according to the two types of cultures. The countries start off at a high-context level and, as they move down the levels, they tend to be of a lower context nature. The figure contains the hierarchies of two different sources. There are slight differences but both generally tend to agree on the cultural-context levels of the various countries. Generally, high-context countries and people would include the Maoris of New Zealand, Native Americans and Chinese,

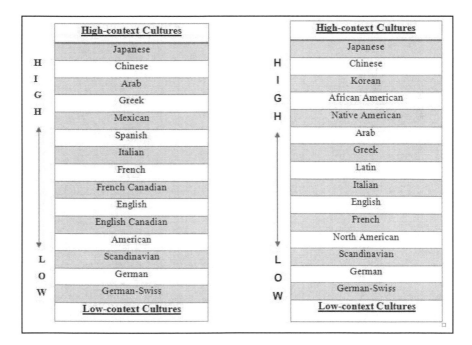

Fig. 1. High- and low-context nationalities scale according to culture (Left diagram [7]; Right diagram [5])

Chilean, Iraqi and Japanese people. On the other hand, low-context countries include the United States, Norway, Austria, Germany, Canada, England and Sweden.

Figure 2 displays the communication pattern that is followed by high- and low-context cultures. A message that is being transmitted needs to be explicitly explained in low-context cultures. The higher the cultural-context of a culture, the more implicit the transmitted message becomes.

In terms of Figure 2, Switzerland is the lowest cultural-context culture on the high- and low-context continuum. Thus, the transmitted message here will be in its most explicit form. On the other hand, Japan is the highest cultural-context culture on the high- and low-context continuum. Hence, the transmitted message there will be in its most implicit form.

If countries from Africa were to be positioned on the "Communication patterns" diagram, they would reside somewhere within the red circle. This conclusion was reached by an investigation of the relevant literature.

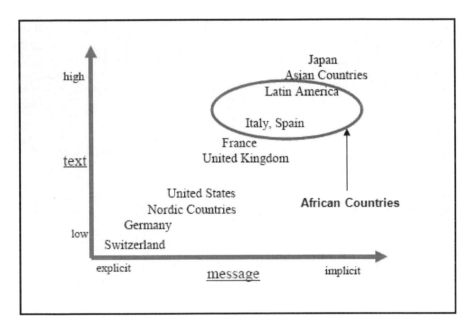

Fig. 2. Communication patterns [10]

Knowledge of where different countries are pitched is important but it is also relevant to highlight web design features when analysing culture-context dimensions.

2.3 Web Design Features of Different Context Countries

By analysing the culture-context dimension in terms of web design, patterns can be identified. These patterns can then be associated with features on a web site, which are preferred in high- or low-context societies respectively. Some of these web design features are summarised in Table 1.

Table 1. High- and Low-context features [11; 12]

High-context features	Low-context features
Polychronic aspects of time	Monochronic aspects of time
Multiple use of images and/or banners	Less use of images and/or banners
Multiple use of links (external links promote a collectivist nature, working together)	Less use of links
Use of Flash features	Little use of Flash features
Being polite and indirect	Being direct and even confrontational
Create a friendly relationship with the customer (soft-sell approach)	Sales orientation (hard-sell approach)
Use of aesthetics to elicit emotion (harmony, beauty, nature, art, designs)	Direct communication (focus on rank and prestige, superlatives, terms and conditions)

One can better comprehend the difference in web design preferences by examining a web site in terms of five parameters. These parameters are displayed in Table 2. The use of each parameter is assessed by means of a high- or low-context culture.

Table 2. Observations of the HC and LC tendencies in terms of parameters [13]

Parameter	Tendency in high-context cultures	Tendency in low-context cultures
Animation	High use of animation, especially in connection with images of moving people	Lower use of animation, mainly reserved for highlighting effects e.g. of text
Promotion of values	Images promote values characteristic of collectivistic societies	Images promote values characteristic of individualistic societies
Individuals separate or together with the product	Featured images depict products and merchandise in use by individuals	Images portray lifestyles of individuals, with or without a direct emphasis on the use of products or merchandise
Level of transparency	Links promote an exploratory approach to navigation on the website; process oriented	Clear and redundant cues in connection with navigation on a website; goal oriented
Linear vs. parallel navigation on the website	Many sidebars and menus, opening of new browser windows for each new page	Few sidebars and menus, constant opening in same browser window

There are a number of values and characteristics that are useful to consider when designing software products for both low- and high-context cultures. The values are withdrawn from the society itself and are determined by the way a culture perceives and understands life.

3 Methodology

As the primary objective of this research is to make suggestions that could contribute to a more effective and usable e-Government website in the specific countries taking into account the cultural context of the society it is serving. The focus has been on the selected populations with the emphasis on culture context as a cultural dimension. In order to measure the cultural profile of the selected populations, a questionnaire focussing on the following aspects has been used:

- the culture-related behaviour of citizens in general Internet usage
- the culture-related behaviour of citizens when using their countries government website
- the general culture-related behaviour of (not related to ICT in any way).

Thus this is a qualitative research study with the aim to elicit experiences from different cultures around the world to determine their cultural context of the use of their e-government websites.

A phased approach has been followed to gather information for the purpose of this research as the study has the potential to be expanded into a very large study.

Phase I

- Identification of participating countries
- Distribution of online survey to sample populations
- Analysis of survey data
- Preparation of survey report
- Presentation of findings

Phase II

- Expert review of participating countries' sites by design experts
- Analysis of expert reviews
- Preparation of report on expert review
- Data triangulation (which may require interviews with citizens from the different countries)
- Presentation of findings

For the purpose of this paper only data from phase one was analysed and discussed.

A sample is a representative part of the targeted population that is methodologically selected to participate in a study [14]. To address the purpose of this study purposive sampling has been applied when sampling the various participants.

According to Babbie [15] purposive sampling involves the selection of the units to be observed on the basis of your own judgment about which ones will be the most useful or representative. Purposive sampling is also called judgmental sampling. Participants were therefore selected to fully represent both high- and low-cultural context countries through purposive sampling. For this paper two groups were selected, one representing the low-context culture and included the countries: Germany, Finland, France and Scotland and the other group (low-context cultures) consisted of South Africa, India, China and Zimbabwe.

A total of ten participants' results have been analysed. Five participants have been selected from each type of culture, low- and high-context respectively. The questionnaire has four main questions (or parts):

- Question 1: Biographical information.
- Question 2: Culture-related behaviour in Internet usage. In this section, the focus is on the participants' preferences' when using any type of web site except government ones.
- Question 3: Culture-related behaviour: government websites. In this section, the focus is on the participants' preferences when using government web sites in particular.
- Question 4: General culture-related behaviour. The focus in this section is on the participants' cultural behaviour within their society.

Most of the items in sections 2 and 3 of the questionnaire focus on particular web design aspects. These items are therefore grouped according to the task or feature that they examine. However, a number of items are not incorporated into any groups. Rather, they test specific aspects of web design, as well as the preferences of the users when using the web sites. For the purpose of this paper, only items that belong to a particular group will be discussed. Consequently, individual items are excluded in this analysis. As for the items in section 4, they all are integrated into a particular group, so they are all analysed. In terms of section 1, the biographical information section, the users' country and home language is specified.

4 Method of Analysis

The methodology in which the analysis was conducted is based on four steps:

1. The participant's country will first be determined in terms of culture context: high or low.
2. Each item of the survey is examined for each participant according to their culture context. Once it is known, if the country is a high- or low-context culture, the answer to each item is already anticipated. The majority of answers should lean towards one side of the scale (either "Agree" and "Strongly Agree" or "Disagree" and "Strongly Disagree").
3. The results of each item for each particular user are now recorded. The next step is to measure the items within their corresponding groups. Most of the groups will have at least three items within them. In some of the cases there are only two items in a group.
4. Based on the overall assessment of the items that represent a group, the tendency must be classified: high- or low-context. Additionally, the level of

support for this tendency must also be provided. The culture-context tendency of a group can be moderately or strongly supported.

It has to be noted that in the case where there was no answer for a particular item it was not included into the assessment of a group (if it belonged to a particular group). For a tendency to be strongly supported it is required that it meets at least 2/3 of the requirements for the culture-context group it represents. For example, in the case where a participant from a high-context culture is being assessed, at least two out of three items in a group should lean towards the high-context scale. Moderate support is used when a participant has 1/3 of the requirements but for the other two items the answer "Not Sure" was selected.

5   Participants in Low-Context Countries

The results from the five participants representing low-context countries will now be presented. The countries represented include:

- Germany (corresponds to row 4 of the results in Excel)
- Finland (corresponds to row 14 of the results in Excel)
- Finland (corresponds to row 16 of the results in Excel)
- France (corresponds to row 21 of the results in Excel)
- Scotland (corresponds to row 21 of the results in Excel)

Each participant has results included in three different tables. For each of those tables the specific user is identified by the number in the "User "column. This number corresponds to the same person in these tables. The results from the low-context participants will be discussed in the following order:

- Section 2 results (preferences in general web sites)
- Section 3 results (preferences in government web sites)
- Section 4 results (culture characteristics in society)

5.1   Section 2 Results

Table 3. Results on section 2 of survey for the low-context participants

User	Country	Home language	Cognitive groups	Culture-context tendencies	Level of support
1	Germany	German	Accomplishing objectives (e.g. tasks)	High context	Strong
			Finding information	Low context	Strong
			Better understanding of content (multimedia or text)	Low context	Strong

Table 3. (*Continued*)

			Amount of multimedia content and colour use	Low context	Strong
2	Finland	Finnish	Accomplishing objectives (e.g. tasks)	High context	Strong
			Finding information	Low context	Strong
			Better understanding of content (multimedia or text)	Low context	Strong
			Amount of multimedia content and colour use	Low context	Strong
3	Finland	Finnish	Accomplishing objectives (e.g. tasks)	High context	Strong
			Finding information	Combination of high and low context	
			Better understanding of content (multimedia or text)	Low context	Strong
			Amount of multimedia content and colour use	Low context	Strong
4	France	English and French	Accomplishing objectives (e.g. tasks)	High context	Strong
			Finding information	Combination of high and low context	
			Better understanding of content (multimedia or text)	Low context	Moderate
			Amount of multimedia content and colour use	Low context	Strong
5	Scotland	English	Accomplishing objectives (e.g. tasks)	High context	Strong
			Finding information	Low context	Moderate
			Better understanding of content (multimedia or text)	Low context	Strong
			Amount of multimedia content and colour use	Low context	Strong

Overall, the results indicate that the low-context participants did prefer low-context features for their general Internet usage (this includes all types of web sites except for the government ones). The key points from Table 3 are the following:

- Participants 1, 2 and 5 demonstrated preferences towards low-context styles for three out of the four cognitive groups that were assessed.
- Participants 3 and 4 demonstrated preferences towards low-context styles for two out of the four cognitive groups that were assessed. For the third cognitive group, they preferred a combination of low- and high-context styles (finding information).
- All participants demonstrated preferences towards high-context styles for one group that was assessed (accomplishing objectives).
- Participants 2 and 3 were both from Finland. They had a different preference for one of the cognitive groups that was assessed (finding information). The one preferred a low-context style while the other preferred a combination of low- and high context styles.

5.2 Section 3 Results

Table 4. Results on section 3 of survey for the low-context participants

User	Country	Home language	Cognitive groups	Culture-context tendencies	Level of support
1	Germany	German	Accomplishing objectives (e.g. tasks)	High context	Strong
			Finding information	Low context	Strong
			Better understanding of content (multimedia or text)	Low context	Strong
			Amount of multimedia content and colour use	Low context	Strong
2	Finland	Finnish	Accomplishing objectives (e.g. tasks)	Low context	Strong
			Finding information	Low context	Strong
			Better understanding of content (multimedia or text)	Low context	Moderate
			Amount of multimedia content and colour use	Low context	Strong
3	Finland	Finnish	Accomplishing objectives (e.g. tasks)	High context	Strong
			Finding information	Low context	Strong
			Better understanding of content (multimedia or text)	Low context	Strong
			Amount of multimedia content and colour use	Low context	Strong

Table 4. (*Continued*)

4	France	English and French	Accomplishing objectives (e.g. tasks)	High context	Strong
			Finding information	Low context	Strong
			Better understanding of content (multimedia or text)	Low context	Moderate
			Amount of multimedia content and colour use	Low context	Strong
5	Scotland	English	Accomplishing objectives (e.g. tasks)	High context	Strong
			Finding information	Low context	Moderate
			Better understanding of content (multimedia or text)	Low context	Strong
			Amount of multimedia content and colour use	Low context	Strong

Overall, the results indicate that the low-context participants did prefer more low-context features on government web sites than they did for their general Internet usage. The key points from Table 4 are the following:

- Participants 1, 3, 4 and 5 demonstrated preferences towards low-context styles for three out of the four cognitive groups that were assessed.
- Participant 2 demonstrated preferences towards low-context styles for all of the four cognitive groups that were assessed.
- Participants 1, 3, 4 and 5 demonstrated preferences towards high-context styles for one group that was assessed (accomplishing objectives).
- Participants 2 and 3 were both from Finland. They had a different preference for one of the cognitive groups that was assessed (accomplishing objectives). The one preferred a low-context style while the other preferred a high-context style.

5.3 Section 4 Results

Table 5. Results on section 4 of survey for the low-context participants

User	Country	Home language	Cognitive groups	Culture-context tendencies	Level of support
1	Germany	German	Time (polychronic vs. monochronic)	High context (polychronic)	Strong
			Orientation (long term vs. short term)	High context (long term)	Strong

Table 5. (*Continued*)

			Role in society and predominant values (individualism vs. collectivism)	Low context (individualism)	Strong
			Communication (high-context vs. low context)	Low context	Moderate
2	Finland	Finnish	Time (polychronic vs. monochronic)	High context (polychronic)	Strong
			Orientation (long term vs. short term)	High context (long term)	Strong
			Role in society and predominant values (individualism vs. collectivism)	Low context (individualism)	Strong
			Communication (high-context vs. low context)	High context	Moderate
3	Finland	Finnish	Time (polychronic vs. monochronic)	High context (polychronic)	Strong
			Orientation (long term vs. short term)	Low context (short term)	Strong
			Role in society and predominant values (individualism vs. collectivism)	Low context (individualism)	Strong
			Communication (high-context vs. low context)	Low context	Strong
4	France	English and French	Time (polychronic vs. monochronic)	High context (polychronic)	Strong
			Orientation (long term vs. short term)	High context (long term)	Strong
			Role in society and predominant values (individualism vs. collectivism)	Low context (individualism)	Strong
			Communication (high-context vs. low context)	High context	Strong
5	Scotland	English	Time (polychronic vs. monochronic)	High context (polychronic)	Strong
			Orientation (long term vs. short term)	Low context (short term)	Strong
			Role in society and predominant values (individualism vs. collectivism)	High context (collectivism)	Moderate
			Communication (high-context vs. low context)	High context	Strong

The results from Table 5 contradict the literature which is really sustainable if one considers the number of participants who took part in this study. Overall, the results indicate that the low-context participants were more high-context in terms of their cultural characteristics within their society. The key points from Table 5 are the following:

- Participants 2, 4 and 5 demonstrated preferences towards low-context styles for one out of the four cognitive groups that were assessed.
- Participant 1demonstrated preferences towards low-context styles for two out of the four cognitive groups that were assessed.
- Participant 3 demonstrated preferences towards low-context styles for three out of the four cognitive groups that were assessed.
- Participants 2 and 3 were both from Finland. They had a different preference for two of the cognitive groups that was assessed (orientation and communication). The one preferred a low-context style for both groups while the other preferred high-context styles respectively.

6 Participants in High-Context Countries

The results from the five participants representing high-context countries will now be presented. The countries represented include:

- South Africa (corresponds to row 6 of the results in Excel)
- India (corresponds to row 5 of the results in Excel)
- China (corresponds to row 9 of the results in Excel)
- Zimbabwe (corresponds to row 11 of the results in Excel)
- South Africa (corresponds to row 7 of the results in Excel)

Each participant has results included in three different tables. For each of those tables the specific user is identified by the number in the "User "column. This number corresponds to the same person in these tables. The results from the high-context participants will be discussed in the following order:

- Section 2 results (preferences in general web sites)
- Section 3 results (preferences in government web sites)
- Section 4 results (culture characteristics in society)

6.1 Section 2 Results

Table 6. Results on section 2 of survey for the high-context participants

User	Country	Home language	Cognitive groups	Culture-context tendencies	Level of support
6	South Africa	Afrikaans	Accomplishing objectives (e.g. tasks)	High context	Strong
			Finding information	High context	Strong
			Better understanding of content (multimedia or text)	High context	Strong

Table 6. (*Continued*)

			Amount of multimedia content and colour use	Low context	Strong
7	India	Tamil	Accomplishing objectives (e.g. tasks)	Low context	Strong
			Finding information	High context	Strong
			Better understanding of content (multimedia or text)	Low context	Strong
			Amount of multimedia content and colour use	High context	Strong
8	China	Chinese	Accomplishing objectives (e.g. tasks)	Low context	Strong
			Finding information	Low context	Moderate
			Better understanding of content (multimedia or text)	High context	Moderate
			Amount of multimedia content and colour use	Low context	Strong
9	Zimbabwe	Ndebele	Accomplishing objectives (e.g. tasks)	Combination of high and low context	
			Finding information	Combination of high and low context	
			Better understanding of content (multimedia or text)	Combination of high and low context	
			Amount of multimedia content and colour use	High context	Strong
10	South Africa	Afrikaans	Accomplishing objectives (e.g. tasks)	High context	Strong
			Finding information	Low context	Strong
			Better understanding of content (multimedia or text)	Low context	Moderate
			Amount of multimedia content and colour use	Combination of high and low context	

Overall, the results indicate that the high-context participants did have a slight preference towards more high-context features for their general Internet usage (this includes all types of web sites except for the government ones). The key points from Table 6 are the following:

- Participant 6 demonstrated preferences towards high-context styles for three out of the four cognitive groups that were assessed.
- Participant 7 demonstrated preferences towards high-context styles for two out of the four cognitive groups that were assessed.
- Participant 8 demonstrated preferences towards high-context styles for one of the four cognitive groups that were assessed.
- Participants 9 and 10 in general demonstrated preferences towards a combination of high-and low-context context styles for the four cognitive groups that were assessed.
- Participants 6 and 10 were both from South Africa. They had different preferences for three of the four cognitive groups that was assessed (finding information, better understanding of content and amount of multimedia content and colour use). Participant 6 preferred high-context styles for finding information and better understanding content. Participant 10 had opposite views, preferring low-context styles respectively. In terms of the cognitive group focusing on multimedia and colour use, participant 6 preferred low-context styles, while participant 10 preferred a combination of high- and low-context styles.

6.2   Section 3 Results

Table 7. Results on section 3 of survey for the high-context participants

User	Country	Home language	Cognitive groups	Culture-context tendencies	Level of support
6	South Africa	Afrikaans	Accomplishing objectives (e.g. tasks)	Low context	Strong
			Finding information	Low context	Strong
			Better understanding of content (multimedia or text)	High context	Moderate
			Amount of multimedia content and colour use	Low context	Moderate
7	India	Tamil	Accomplishing objectives (e.g. tasks)	Low context	Strong
			Finding information	Combination of high and low context	
			Better understanding of content (multimedia or text)	Low context	Moderate

Table 7. (*Continued*)

				Amount of multimedia content and colour use	Combination of high and low context	
8	China	Chinese	Accomplishing objectives (e.g. tasks)	Low context	Strong
			Finding information	Low context	Strong
			Better understanding of content (multimedia or text)	High context	Moderate
			Amount of multimedia content and colour use	Combination of high and low context	
9	Zimbabwe	Ndebele	Accomplishing objectives (e.g. tasks)	Low context	Strong
			Finding information	Combination of high and low context	
			Better understanding of content (multimedia or text)	Combination of high and low context	
			Amount of multimedia content and colour use	Low context	Strong
10	South Africa	Afrikaans	Accomplishing objectives (e.g. tasks)	High context	Strong
			Finding information	Low context	Moderate
			Better understanding of content (multimedia or text)	High context	Moderate
			Amount of multimedia content and colour use	Low context	Moderate

Overall, the results indicate that the high-context participants did prefer more low-context features on government web sites than they did for their general Internet usage. This contradicts the literature. The key points from Table 7 are the following:

- Participant 7 and 9 demonstrated preferences towards high-context styles for none of the four cognitive groups that were assessed. However, they each preferred a combination of high- and low-context styles for two of the groups respectively.
- Participants 6 and 8 demonstrated preferences towards high-context styles for one out of the four cognitive groups that were assessed.
- Participant 10 demonstrated preferences towards high-context styles for two out of the four cognitive groups that were assessed.

- Participants 6 and 10 were both from South Africa. They had different preferences for only one of the four cognitive groups that were assessed (accomplishing objectives). Participant 6 preferred a low-context style, while participant 10 preferred a high-context style.

6.3 Section 4 Results

Table 8. Results on section 4 of survey for the high-context participants

User	Country	Home language	Cognitive groups	Culture-context tendencies	Level of support
6	South Africa	Afrikaans	Time (polychronic vs. monochronic)	High context (polychronic)	Strong
			Orientation (long term vs. short term)	High context (long term)	Strong
			Role in society and predominant values (individualism vs. collectivism)	Low context (individualism)	Strong
			Communication (high-context vs. low context)	High context	Strong
7	India	Tamil	Time (polychronic vs. monochronic)	High context (polychronic)	Strong
			Orientation (long term vs. short term)	Low context (short term)	Strong
			Role in society and predominant values (individualism vs. collectivism)	High context (collectivism)	Strong
			Communication (high-context vs. low context)	Low context	Strong
8	China	Chinese	Time (polychronic vs. monochronic)	Low context (monochronic)	Strong
			Orientation (long term vs. short term)	Combination of high and low context	
			Role in society and predominant values (individualism vs. collectivism)	Low context (individualism)	Strong
			Communication (high-context vs. low context)	High context	Strong

Table 8. (*Continued*)

9	Zimbabwe	Ndebele	Time (polychronic vs. monochronic)	High context (polychronic)	Strong
			Orientation (long term vs. short term)	High context (long term)	Strong
			Role in society and predominant values (individualism vs. collectivism)	Low context (individualism)	Strong
			Communication (high-context vs. low context)	Low context	Moderate
10	South Africa	Afrikaans	Time (polychronic vs. monochronic)	High context (polychronic)	Strong
			Orientation (long term vs. short term)	Low context (short term)	Strong
			Role in society and predominant values (individualism vs. collectivism)	Low context (individualism)	Strong
			Communication (high-context vs. low context)	Low context	Strong

There is a contradiction of the literature once again for this section of results. Overall, the results indicate that the high-context participants did have a slight preference towards more low-context cultural characteristics within their society. The key points from Table 8 are the following:

- Participant 6 demonstrated preferences towards high-context styles for three out of the four cognitive groups that were assessed.
- Participants 7 and 9 demonstrated preferences towards high-context styles for two out of the four cognitive groups that were assessed.
- Participants 8 and 10 demonstrated preferences towards high-context styles for one out of the four cognitive groups that were assessed.
- Participants 6 and 10 were both from South Africa. They had different preferences for two of the four cognitive groups that were assessed (orientation and communication). Participant 6 preferred high-context styles for both, while participant 10 preferred low-context styles respectively.

7 Conclusion

A total of six tables (Tables 3 – 8) were used to display some of the results from the pilot study. Tables 3, 4 and 5 show the preferences of the low-context participants and

Tables 6, 7 and 8 those of the high-context participants. From the six tables, there were three that contradicted the literature:

- Table 3 focused on the low-context participants preferences' when using any type of web site except government ones. The results did not contradict the literature.
- Table 4 focused on the low-context participants preferences' when using government web sites. The results did not contradict the literature.
- Table 5 focused on the low-context participants' cultural behaviour within their society. The results did contradict the literature.
- Table 6 focused on the high-context participants preferences' when using any type of web site except government ones. The results did not contradict the literature.
- Table 7 focused on the high-context participants preferences' when using government web sites. The results did contradict the literature.
- Table 8 focused on the high-context participants' cultural behaviour within their society. The results did contradict the literature.

There are two interesting facts which arise from the initial results. The first is that the high-context participants changed their preferences when using government web sites. Although they preferred high-context styles for their general Internet usage, this was not the case for government web sites. In this environment they preferred more low-context styles. The second is that in terms of the participants cultural behaviours the opposite results of what was expected occurred. The high-context participants had characteristics which were more representative of low-context cultures and vice versa.

The results may have been impacted by the fact that most of the participants had IT related occupations. The other majority occupation was from the education sector. High-context styles tend to contradict the commonly accepted guidelines and principles for web design. These guidelines relate more to low-context preferences. Therefore, the high-context participants may have been influenced by these types of guidelines, thus, preferring low-context styles. In other words, the low-context styles might rather be what are expected of the high-context users to apply or expect on web sites and not actually what they would prefer. This can be observed from the results of the participants from India and China, two countries classified as one of the most high-context. They had preferences towards low-context styles in a number of cases which one would not expect. These results are pertinent for website developers to consider when designing the specific type of country's e-government websites.

In order to get more accurate results, the use of inferential statistics is necessary. This will assist in determining statistically and practically significant differences between the participants from the two types of cultures by making use of single sample t-tests, Pairwise t-tests and effect sizes. However, a much larger sample of participants will be required for each of the cultures: high- and low-context. Another factor is that the participants do not have a high-level of understanding regarding web design practices. As mentioned previously, this may impact the results of high-context participants, who are required to follow web design principles that are better suited to the preferences of low-context individuals.

References

[1] Hofstede, G.: Geert Hofstede Cultural Dimensions (1987-2003), http://www. geert-hofstede.com (retrieved July 02, 2009)

[2] Hall, E.T.: The silent Language. Doubleday, New York (1959)

[3] ChangingMinds.org. Hall's cultural factors (2002-2007), http://www. changingminds.org/explanations/culture/hall_culture.htm (retrieved November 09, 2009)

[4] Ford, G.: Researching the effects of culture on usability. Unpublished MSc. Dissertation, UNISA (2005)

[5] Samovar, L., Porter, R., McDaniel, E.: Communication between cultures, 6th edn. Holly Allen, Belmont (2007)

[6] Samovar, L., Porter, R.: Communication between cultures, 5th edn. Holly J. Allen, Belmont (2004)

[7] O'Hara-Devereaux, M., Johansen, R.: Transcending cultural barriers: Context, relationships, and time (2000), from the World Wide Web http://www.csub.edu/TLC/options/resources/handouts/fac_dev/c ulturalbarries.html (retrieved July 25, 2007)

[8] Timbrook, L.: Mid frame: High/low context cultures (2001), from the World Wide Web http://www.colostate.edu/Depts/Speech/rccs/theory63.htm (retrieved July 2, 2007)

[9] LeBaron, M.: Beyond Intractability.org: Communication tools for understanding cultural differences (2003), from the World Wide Web http://www.beyondintractability.org/essay/communication_tools (retrieved May 20, 2007)

[10] Köszegi, S., Vetschera, R., Kersten, G.E.: National cultural differences in the use and perception of Internet-based NSS: Does high or low context matter? (2003) from the World Wide Web http://www.interneg.concordia.ca/views/bodyfiles/paper/2003/ 09.pdf (retrieved January, 30, 2008)

[11] Sing, N., Matuso, H.: Measuring cultural adaption on the Web: A content analytical study of US and Japanese websites. Journal of Business Research 57(8), 864–872 (2004), from the World Wide Web http://www.linkinghub.elsevier.com/retrieve/pii/S01482963020 04824 (retrieved October 20, 2007)

[12] Gygi, K.F., Spyridakis, J.H.: Developing a cultural model to support website localization: A case study of Uzbek school websites (2007), from the World Wide Web http://www.uwtc.washington.edu/research/pubs/jspyridakis/Cul tural_Model_Web_Site_Localization.pdf (retrieved September 16, 2007)

[13] Wurtz, E.: Intercultural communication on websites: A cross-cultural analysis of websites from high-context cultures and low-context cultures. Journal of Computer-Mediated Communication 11, 274–299 (2006)

[14] Cooper, D.R., Schindler, P.S.: Business Research Methods. 8th edn. McGraw-Hill/Irwin. Avenue of the Americas, New York (2003)

[15] Babbie, E.: The practice of social research. Wadsworth, Belmont (2005)

Improving Public Administrations via Law Modeling and BPR

Aaron Ciaghi and Adolfo Villafiorita

Fondazione Bruno Kessler, via Sommarive 14 Povo (TN), Italy

Abstract. *Semantic Web* technologies can be used to produce conceptual representations of legal documents and to perform reasoning on the information that they contain. At the same time, Business Process Re-engineering is being applied more frequently to optimize the procedures of Public Administrations. While the existing literature on tools and methodologies to analyze, model and manipulate legal documents is extensive, there is a lack of a comprehensive tool that allows for a complete analysis of laws in all their aspect. In this paper we propose the design of a modeling framework to support the law-making process, facilitating the participation of people without a jurisprudence background to the editing of regulations.

1 Introduction

Semantic annotations and interchange formats for laws have raised significant interest. In fact, enriching legal documents with semantic information can greatly aid the reasoning on the statements contained in laws, as well as favor indexing and interchange of the document. In addition, XML has become the *de facto* standard for legal documents authored by the legislative bodies of several countries, including the House of Representatives of the United States of America, the African Union's Parliament and several European governments [5]. Moreover, a Legal Knowledge Interchange Format (LKIF) [6] is the indispensable tool to achieve interoperability among the members of transnational institutions such as the European Union. It is not surprising that the definition of such LKIF is one of the top priorities of the European Union to connect their member countries' Public Administrations [5]. See [1, 2, 3, 4] for further details.

At the same time, the use of Business Process Re-engineering (BPR) has become one of the recent trends to support Public Administrations in redesigning their processes, reducing their costs and improving citizens' participation [7, 8]. There is however a need to link procedures to the regulations by which they are defined and directed. Any implementation of a re-engineered (or a new) process requires a parallel action on both the redesign of processes and on the introduction of law changes. This is to give analysts the ability to understand the impact on laws of a process redesign.

In this paper we propose a *law modeling framework* – called VLPM 2.0 – that leverages existing systems for legal knowledge representation and interchange in

R. Popescu-Zeletin et al. (Eds.): AFRICOMM 2010, LNICST 64, pp. 69–78, 2011.
© Institute for Computer Sciences, Social Informatics and Telecommunications Engineering 2011

order to provide a way to better understand legal documents. Our ultimate goal is that of supporting the law-making process by:

1. Facilitating the participation of people without a jurisprudence background to the editing of regulations.
2. Providing effective means to comprehend the law.
3. Provide a way to make changes to the law and keep track of the dependencies between textual resources (i.e. legal documents and other documentation of a PA procedure) and models.

Specifically, we focus on documents that define, regulate or in some way affect procedures (e.g. Public Administration procedures, company policies that need to comply with certain regulations). This category of legal documents is usually the one in which functional analysts are more interested.

Our framework addresses the needs of three potential users:

- CITIZENS, who want to understand laws, procedures and legal documents in general without any technical or legal expertise.
- FUNCTIONAL ANALYSTS, who analyze the processes in PAs or who need to understand the legal requirements for some (usually IT) system.
- JURISTS, who are in charge of designing and editing a piece of legislation. They need to be able to easily visualize and navigate the document as well as be able to track past changes and dependencies to other documents.

The approach that we present in this paper is of particular interest for the developed world as well as developing countries. As the Report of the 2009 World e-Parliament Conference [16] points out, the latter scenario represents an easier deployment environment for legal ICT-based services due to a usually less saturated body of laws. Moreover, the young democracies of the developing world could greatly benefit from an approach that takes into consideration ICTs in laws since the beginning.

2   Related Work

ICT-based services have become pervasive in modern societies and, as a result, parliaments are relying at different degrees on complex information systems to support their operations. Several works aim at improving and modernizing Parliaments and Public Administrations by providing solutions typical of ICT. These are mainly (usually XML-based) representation formats for legal documents and information systems.

The work presented in this paper uses AKOMA NTOSO XML [1] as format for the representation of input legal documents. AKOMA NTOSO is a project developed by UN/DESA for African parliaments and it includes a schema for the markup of legal texts. This format is designed to achieve interoperability between parliaments and is thus generic and pattern based in order to support different legal systems and document structures. Other markup formats and information systems are described in [5].

In the recent years, the interest towards linguistic and semantic technologies for the representation of legal knowledge has increased. The most notable endeavor in this direction is the Legal Knowledge Interchange Format (LKIF) and its related LKIF-core and LKIF-extended ontologies [6]. This is the main product of the European ESTRELLA Project [5] and it is intended to serve two purposes:

- Provide reusable ontologies for the development of legal knowledge management systems.
- Provide an interchange format for existing legal knowledge representation languages.

Visual modeling approaches have been applied to the legal field by other related projects. The most common reason to model legal information is compliance assessment of business processes. See for example jUCMNav [13], which is used to evaluate the compliance of processes to legal requirements and has a method to establish traceability links between elements such as goals and procedures [14].

While our focus is on the business processes of Public Administrations, legal documents do not usually contain only procedural information. High level principles and rules play a crucial role in regulating and motivating processes.

Our framework will be primarily based on the concepts of two approaches that are complementary in representing these two aspects of legal documents [11]:

- VLPM [10] uses UML to model the processes defined by a law, semi-automatically extracting them from a legal text marked with the NormeIn-Rete XML tags [3]. The methodology it enforces strictly separates the actors, the entities and the activities defined in the document and organizes them in a hierarchical fashion. More notably, VLPM supports change management of a law by maintaining the traceability between the text and the model elements. VLPM has been used in the context of the introduction of e-Voting in the Italian autonomous region of Friuli Venezia Giulia in 2007.
- NOMOS [9] is a goal-oriented approach to effectively capture high-level principles in terms of goal realization for requirements guided by satisfiability of normative propositions obtained from rules embedded in a law. This approach, based on the i* framework [12], aims at applying goal reasoning to legal knowledge in order to model the aspects of a legal document that do not represent procedures.

This paper presents a possible framework architecture to implement the integration of the two approaches presented above. The integration between of the two methodologies is justified by [18] as a way to achieve a legally correct representation of a procedure.

Although outside the scope of this work, formal verification of processes [15] is an aspect worthy of notice as it could be integrated into the law modeling process as future work.

3   VLPM 2.0

In this section we describe a law modeling framework – VLPM 2.0 – to support re-engineering of Public Administration procedures. We first introduce the issues of modeling information contained in laws. We then present an ontology for business process concepts that we use as interchange format for our modeling and finally we discuss the components of our framework. Although this chapter (and this paper) focus on the extraction of procedural information from legal documents, our approach supports any type of document from which information relevant to the domain being model can be found.

3.1   Modeling Processes and Other Aspects of Laws

For anyone without a jurisprudence background, laws are extremely difficult to understand, mainly due to the complexity of the legal language and the intricate system of dependencies in which they exist. Furthermore, the application of laws is subject to the *interpretation* of a set of documents and thus, to a certain degree, subjective. Despite the fact that processes are defined in laws usually written for that purpose, they always depend on a set of laws that define principles and rules to be followed. This requires a holistic approach to law modeling.

If the text of a norm is well formed[1], it organizes its statements by their type, generally using the following three classes (see [17] for a more detailed discussion):

- *Constitutive Rules*: rules that answer the question "what is X?". They define abstract and concrete entities such as concepts, actors, institutions, roles, competences, attributes, etc. that did not exist before the promulgation of the law.
- *Instructional Rules*: rules that answer the question "what to do?". They give prescriptions that fix duties with respect to given goals.
- *Procedural Rules*: rules that answer the question "how to do X?". They define formal obligations and model formal actions.

In general, a legal text is an unordered mix of rules of these three classes. An expert is needed to classify each paragraph, isolate the procedural statements from the others and determine the sequentiality of the described activities and events, as well as the involved actors. Deciding the degree of formality used to model legally defined processes is not an easy task. Laws are (or at least should be) formally written in order to avoid ambiguities and this should intuitively suggest that a formal modeling language is required. However, process models should be easily understandable and visualizable by users with non-technical backgrounds. We consider UML-AD (UML Activity Diagrams) and BPMN as two candidate languages that fit this description as they are both based on the semantics of Petri Nets, thus fulfilling the requirement of formality, and they are both visualizable and easily understandable.

---

[1] Usually this means following the national directives for the correct drafting of laws.

The categorization of laws presented above leads to the observation that business process models are not sufficient to represent all the aspects of a law. Legal documents, in fact, often define complex constraints that affect processes and that cannot be modeled as sequences of actions.

3.2   Data Representation and Traceability

Enriching the text of a law with semantic information has many advantages, among which that of allowing reasoning on the legal concepts in the text. The LKIF-core ontology [6] has been developed with this purpose in mind. However, since it has been designed as part of a generic architecture for legal knowledge systems, the support that it gives to process modeling is at a very high level, while the sub-ontology of legal entities is much more detailed.

In order to be able to add semantic information about the business processes described in legal texts, we developed an ontology that extends the concepts in LKIF-core with a business process meta-model that borrows several entities from the BPMN meta-model [19]. In this way, we added some concepts that partially overlap with LKIF-core entities but that more effectively address our needs. Our ontology is not a specification of the BPMN meta-model in OWL. We instead abstracted the core entities of a business process from the BPMN meta-model, obtaining a smaller but more generic ontology, in the sense that a set of instances of the classes in our ontology could be easily transformed to BPMN as well as UML-AD.

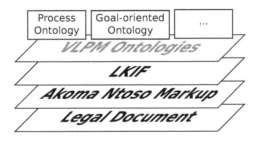

Fig. 1. VLPM 2.0 layered approach to legal knowledge representation

For our framework, we envisaged a layered approach to knowledge representation, as depicted in Figure 1.

The first level above the raw document is represented by AKOMA NTOSO markup, that helps us structuring the text and adding references to external ontology elements. The layer above the markup consists of an RDF representation of the model (made of instances of LKIF and VLPM 2.0 ontologies). We use the referencing mechanism of the AKOMA NTOSO schema to tag fragments of texts so that they become linked – where relevant – to elements of this model. Notice that our framework aims at being general and, in fact, Figure 1 shows that it is possible to have multiple ontologies to represent different aspects of a law.

Figure 2 depicts the core classes of our ontology that represent Business Process entities. The diagram includes (shaded) classes from the LKIF ontologies to highlight the connection between Business Process concepts and legal concepts.

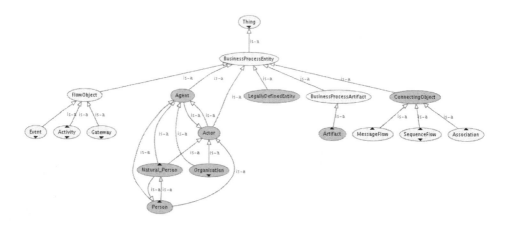

Fig. 2. VLPM 2.0 Ontology Business Process Entity classes

By using an intermediate representation in RDF of the model data, using instances of the classes of our ontology, we can achieve traceability between the text and the models. Figure 3 details how this traceability is maintained (the diagram refers to Business Process modeling). References to external resources are "declared" in the header of an AKOMA NTOSO document as Top Level Class (TLC) References. We make them point to instances of classes of our ontology (instances of Business Process Entities in the case of the figure). An inline reference points to a TLC reference using its local ID. Each TLC reference has a URI that points to an entity in the RDF store, thus allowing an inline reference to be connected to such entity. Backwards traceability is achieved by using the *defined_ by* object relationship of the VLPM 2.0 ontology from the business process entity to a *Legal_ Source* with the URI of the inline reference. In the same way, by making sure that the URI of the business process entity in the RDF Store is the same in the model (that is usually written in XML/XMI), we achieve RDF-model traceability. The *modeled_ by* object property is provided to link entities to model elements that don't have the same URI. This is due to the fact that a model is the result of a transformation of (part of) the RDF store to another notation that can have an incompatible URI schema.

3.3   Framework Components

Law modeling with VLPM 2.0 is a process in four phases:

1. *Markup*: in this phase a legal document (or a set of legal documents) in AKOMA NTOSO XML format is marked with tags that identify business process entities, namely actors, activities, artifacts, events.
2. *Transformation*: in this phase the objects in the RDF store are transformed to a suitable representation in a modeling notation (e.g. BPMN for process modeling). This transformation must be performed in such a way that the already established links with text fragments are maintained.
3. *Modeling*: in this phase the analysts use conventional modeling tools to work with the model(s) obtained at the end of the transformation.
4. *Change Management*: this last phase involves identifying the changes made to the model(s) and comparing them with their original version in order to evaluate the impact of changes to the model on the laws. This can be used to generate skeletons of amendments (in AKOMA NTOSO XML) to be evaluated and edited by stakeholders with legal expertise.

We envisaged four components of our framework to support these four phases:

- *Editor*: this component is a customization of Bungeni Editor[2] that adds UI elements and functions to mark up part of the text and link them to instances of ontology classes. We designed a Model Element Editor to graphically manipulate elements in the RDF store from within the editor that is called when a portion of text is marked as relevant for the analyst.
- *RDF Store*: this component stores all the model information and the traceability links using a semantic notation.
- *Transformer*: this component is an extension of the Transformer Server of Bungeni Editor. Bungeni Editor relies on a XSLT engine that runs as a HTTP service and that is integrated via a REST API. An interface is provided to extend the transformer with new target formats. The role of the transformer is that of converting the document into an XML file and of translating the content of the RDF store to formats understandable by modeling tools. For this reason, extensions for this module must be implemented for each target modeling tool.
- *Change Manager*: this is the module of VLPM 2.0 that manages the changes in models and provide the means to evaluate the impact of such changes to the current law. It must be implemented as a plugin of a modeling tool or as a standalone application that takes as input the model. The Change Manager must be able to identify the changes the model has undergone and navigate the links between the modified model elements and the related text fragments. The module must then visually show the impact of such modifications and allow the creation of a template of a new amendment to the current law.

---

[2] The official editor for AKOMA NTOSO documents, available at
http://code.google.com/p/bungeni-editor/

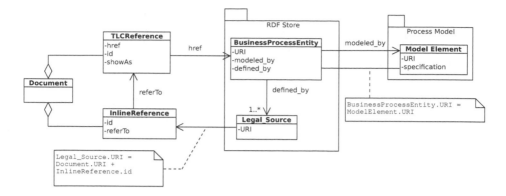

Fig. 3. VLPM 2.0 *Round-trip* Traceability Strategy

4   Conclusions and Future Work

In the last decade parliaments have put a signicant effort into the development of ICT solutions to facilitate the access to legal information. The definition of standards plays a key role in the delivery of services to the citizens but it also paves the way for the development of new tools. This is particularly evidenced by the Africa i-Parliaments Action Plan[3], in which the AKOMA NTOSO XML standard is designed not only to accomodate current users but also future developers of tools for the manipulation of legal documents.

A major issue faced by Public Administrations is the complexity of legislations, in which laws are continously added, amended and repealed, often causing inconsistencies that can go unnoticed even for several decades. This is further complicated by the overlapping of transnational legislation, such as that of the European Union. Besides "technical" challenges, a serious issue is represented by the fact that laws are mainly a product of political representatives, who might have an agenda that does not include facilitating understandability ("obscurity by design"). This would represent the main obstacle to the implementation of formal approaches to law design.

In this paper we have presented a framework that aims at addressing the needs of citizens, analysts (from Public Administrations or companies) and jurists. VLPM 2.0 is an approach based on (graphical) modeling of the contents of the legal documents that regulate a domain. The complete approach can be applied in developing countries and especially in young democracies. In a context in which the legal system is not as complex as in developed countries, designing laws in a formalized way (with the aid of visual modeling) could foster the consistency of the law system and the efficiency of Public Administration. Moreover, facilitating the access to parliamentary information by using semantically rich meta-data and simplified visualizations of laws can signicantly speed up development by increasing the participation of citizens to a true "*e-*"Democracy.

---

[3] http://www.parliaments.info/

Furthermore, this application of VLPM 2.0 could represent an opportunity for "reverse innovation". In fact, while VLPM 2.0 would have to deal with the relatively low complexity of the legal systems of developing countries, such deployment scenario would be a testbed to facilitate the subsequent deployment in more developed and complex environments.

However, in order for this framework to be deployable, several challenges have to be addressed:

- It is necessary to improve the support to different views of the same domain, without disregarding non-procedural information.
- We need to better understand the needs and expectations of jurists, in order to make the framework more usable in a real setting. There is thus a need to carefully design the User Experience of these stakeholders.
- Finally, while the framework aims at being generic, there is a need to formalize the methodology or a set of best practices for law modeling, in order to improve the quality of analysis and re-engineering of legally defined procedures.

References

1. Vitali, F., Zeni, F.: Towards a country-independent data format: the Akoma Ntoso experience. In: Biagioli, C., Francesconi, E., Sartor, G. (eds.) Proceedings of the 5th Legislative XML Workshop, pp. 67–86. European Press Academic Publishing (2007)
2. Boer, A., Winkels, R., Vitali, F.: MetaLex XML and the Legal Knowledge Interchange Format. In: Casanovas, P., Sartor, G., Casellas, N., Rubino, R. (eds.) Computable Models of the Law. LNCS (LNAI), vol. 4884, pp. 21–41. Springer, Heidelberg (2008)
3. Lupo, C., Batini, C.: A Federative Approach to Laws Access by Citizens: The Normeinrete System. In: Traunmüller, R. (ed.) EGOV 2003. LNCS, vol. 2739, pp. 413–416. Springer, Heidelberg (2003)
4. Marchetti, A., Megale, F., Seta, E., Vitali, F.: Using XML as a means to Access Legislative Documents: Italian and Foreign Experiences. SIGAPP Appl. Comput. Rev. (1), 54–62 (2002)
5. ESTRELLA Project Deliverable 3.1: General XML format(s) for legal Sources. CNIPA, MRIPA (2007)
6. Hoekstra, R., Breuker, J., Di Bello, M., Boer, A.: The LKIF Core ontology of basic legal concepts. In: Proceedings of the Workshop on Legal Ontologies and Artificial Intelligence Techniques (2007)
7. Alpar, P., Olbrich, S.: Legal Requirements and Modelling of Processes in e-Government. Electronic Journal of e-Government 3(3), 107–116 (2005)
8. Thaens, M., Bekkers, V., van Duivenboden, H.P.M.: HPM: Business process redesign and public administration: a perfect match? In: Taylor, J.A., Snellen, I.T.M., Zuurmond, A. (eds.) Beyond BPR in Public Administration: An Institutional Transformation in an Information Age, pp. 15–36. IOS Press, Amsterdam (1997)
9. Siena, A., Mylopoulos, J., Perini, A., Susi, A.: The Nomos framework: Modelling requirements compliant with laws. Technical Report TR-0209-SMSP, FBK-Irst (2009), http://disi.unitn.it/asiena/files/TR-0209-SMSP.pdf

10. Ciaghi, A., Mattioli, A., Villafiorita, A.: A tool supported methodology for BPR in Public Administrations. Int. J. of Electronic Governance 3-2, 148–169 (2010)
11. Villafiorita, A., Weldemariam, K., Susi, A., Siena, A.: Modeling and Analysis of Laws using BPR and Goal-oriented framework. FBK-Irst (2010)
12. Yu, E.S.K.: Modelling strategic relationships for process reengineering. University of Toronto, Toronto (1995)
13. Mussbacher, G., Amyot, D.: Goal and Scenario Modeling, Analysis, and Transformation with jUCMNav. In: 31st International Conference on Software Engineering (ICSE 2009), pp. 16–24 (2009)
14. Ghanavati, S., Amyot, D., Peyton, L.: Compliance Analysis Based on a Goal-oriented Requirement Language Evaluation Methodology. In: Proc. of the 17th IEEE Intl. Conf. on Requirements Engineering, pp. 133–142 (2009)
15. Weldemariam, K., Villafiorita, A.: Formal procedural security modeling and analysis. In: Third International Conference on Risks and Security of Internet and Systems, CRiSIS 2008, pp. 249–254 (2008)
16. Global Centre for ICT in Parliament: World e-Parliament Conference Report (2009)
17. Biagioli, C.: Ordinamenti normativi e tipologia delle norme. In: Sartor, G. (ed.) Regole e atti linguistici nel discorso normativo, ch. I, pp. 201–223 (1993) (in Italian)
18. Olbrich, S., Simon, C.: Process Modelling towards e-Government – Visualisation and Semantic Modelling of Legal Regulations as Executable Process Sets. Electronic Journal of e-Government 6(1), 43–54 (2008)
19. White, S., et al.: Business Process Modeling Notation (BPMN) Version 1.0. Business Process Management Initiative (2004)

Adaptation of Mobile Application to Improve Flow of Birth Information from the Community to the District Level

Caroline Ngoma, Marlen Stacey Chawani, and Jo Herstad

University of Oslo, Department of Informatics, P.O. Box 1080 Blindern,
N-0316 Oslo. Norway
{caroline.ngoma,marlene483}@gmail.com, johe@ifi.uio.no

Abstract. This paper presents current practices used by village health workers, traditional birth attendants, health facility workers and district health managers in collection, recording, storing and transferring birth information in the health information system. Envisioned potentials of using mobile application as a tool for data recording, transferring and strengthening the weak support structure have been foreseen to bring improvements in the flow of birth information in the Health Information System.

Keywords: Village health workers, Traditional birth attendants, Health managers, Mobile phones, Supportive supervision, Feedback and Medical birth registration.

1 Introduction

In sub-Saharan countries, studies have pointed out under-reporting of maternal health data; and the data reported indicates a high rate of maternal and child mortality [1, 2]. This situation is prominent in rural communities where many women deliver their children at home assisted by traditional birth attendants. In Tanzania, 46-60 % of births take place in the community [1, 3]. The information about these births may neither be recorded nor reported in the Health Information System (HIS) and these children may live without a trace of their existence. Hence the availability of accurate and complete information on all births within the community is one of the main concerns within the HIS.

Registration of new born children which is the main concern of this study, is done in health facilities where details of a child's birth and his/her medical condition if any or death, and the parents' vital information and medical conditions of the mother if any are captured. This data is useful for epidemiological purposes such as monitoring surveillance of birth defects and other prenatal health problems and for analysing quality assurance on health services related to pregnancy, childbirth and the neonatal period. As such, these records can provide the best answers on the rate of maternal/child/neonatal mortality for a health facility, a community and a country population at large.

R. Popescu-Zeletin et al. (Eds.): AFRICOMM 2010, LNICST 64, pp. 79–92, 2011.
© Institute for Computer Sciences, Social Informatics and Telecommunications Engineering 2011

The objective of this study was to find ways of improving birth registration in the community through facilitating communication of birth information between community health workers in the community, health facility workers in the health facilities and district health managers in the district. To attain this objective, this study will answer the following questions: 1. What are the current practices used by village health workers, traditional birth attendants, health facility workers and health managers in collecting, recording, storing and transferring birth information? 2. What are the opportunities provided by the envisioned mobile application to communicate birth information from the community to the district level?

1.1 Research Context

This is an ongoing research study taking place in Tanzania and Malawi as part of a project aimed at improving the availability and quality of maternal health data in the HIS. The study is taking place in Kibaha and Bagamoyo districts which are located in the Coastal region of Tanzania. This paper presents findings from Kwala ward which is one of the nine wards of Kibaha district. The Kwala ward consists of four villages and it has one dispensary and one health center.

HIS Information Flows. In the health information system, data is collected routinely as well as non-routinely from communities, health facilities (health centers and dispensaries) and hospitals (district, regional, national and referral hospitals). The flow of routine data reporting is bottom-up from the community to the ministry, while provision of support and feedback is from top-down. Figure 1 presents hierarchy of data reporting and provision of support and feedback in the HIS.

Fig. 1. Hierarchy of Health Information System [4]

Mother and Child Health (MCH) Services. At all levels of the HIS, MCH services provided include antenatal care, delivery, postnatal care, child health management, immunisation and family planning with different intensities of specialisation. These services are provided by various groups of health professionals such as nurses, midwives, MCH aides, medical doctors, and clinical officers. Some MCH services are also provided as part of community health services by non-medical professionals such as trained and untrained traditional birth attendants and village health workers. Data on maternal (mother and child) health is collected and recorded hand in hand as the services are provided.

Maternal health data collected at the community level was individual-based data which could be traced back to a particular individual however the identifications used were not unique. The data is then aggregated at the end of the month and/or quarter and reported to the health facility in an aggregated format. At the health facilities individual-based data is also collected and reported in an aggregated format together with the data reported from the community. The aggregated data contains combined sums of individual data; it eliminates presenting data in individual-based format.

This study concentrated on the registration of births/new born babies at the community and health facility levels which is highly related to the process of capturing delivery outcomes for both the child and the mother. In this paper, Community Health Worker (CHW) is used as a group term referring to village health workers and traditional birth attendants.

2 Literature Review

This section presents literature and theoretical concepts on HISs in developing countries in order to show existing practices in data collection, recording and transferring. Theoretical concepts on ways of motivating performance of CHWs in order to improve data reporting are also presented in this section. Furthermore, we present opportunities for using mobile phone applications in HISs.

2.1 Health Information Systems in Developing Countries

In most developing countries, HISs do not function properly especially at the community level which is the main source of data while the main goal of the HIS is to collect complete and accurate data, report it on time and utilise it. To achieve this goal at the community level, Lippeveld [5] argues that, health managers need to find ways of involving CHWs and improving their performance. According to Rowe et al. [6], health managers can promote certain practices among health workers by first understanding "*the existing and often evolving influences that promote desirable and undesirable practices.*" Studies conducted in developing countries indicate that CHWs' performance on desirable practices can be improved by motivating them [7-11].

2.2 Motivating the Performance of CHWs

Motivation is "*an individual's degree of willingness to exert and maintain an effort towards organisational goals*" [9]. For the HIS to be able to collect and report information on births taking place in the community, CHWs need to be highly motivated to fully participate in this exercise because they are closer to the community than health facility workers are. Empirical studies present different approaches that can be adapted to motivate performance of CHWs such as provision of supportive supervision, feedback, incentives, training etc.

Supportive Supervision. Supportive supervision is one of the determining factors of CHWs' success as it provides a way of reducing/avoiding mistakes and updating their knowledge and skills [8, 9, 12]. It is a system whereby supervisors can provide guidance on the technical aspects of the services by going through a checklist. As a way of improving the quality of data collected, HIS need to set up a strong support structure that will ensure provision of reliable and timely support to CHWs in accomplishing their tasks.

For instance, health workers in Kenya and Benin who were rarely and irregularly supervised indicated that "*supervision provides the feeling of being cared for and of appreciation*"[9]. Furthermore, Franco et al. [9] add that good supervision should include "*adequate technical support and feedback, recognition of achievements and good communication.*" These attributes will make supervision a way of motivating health workers and improving desirable work practices in the HIS.

Meaningful Feedback. Provision of meaningful feedback to health workers is a way to showing appreciation and it is one the most important motivating factor [10]. However most CHWs received little or no feedback from their supervisors. In the study conducted in Kenya and Benin, Mathauer & Imhoff [8] indicated that when health workers received feedback, it was based on shortcomings and mistakes on the different aspects of service provision. This kind of feedback was like a punishment to health workers, instead of improving their performance, it demotivated them.

2.3 Mobile Applications in the HIS

The use of mobile applications for health services and information transferring and sharing is rapidly growing in developing countries mainly due to a high diffusion of mobile phones [13, 14]. The use of mobile applications has proven to be beneficial in several areas of health service delivery such as: capturing and transmission of health data on public health programmes and routine epidemiological data from remote clinics to regional health centres [15]; submission of child nutrition data via mobile phone SMS for monitoring children nutrition [16]; capturing patient-level data when providing home-based care to HIV/AIDS patients [17]; and improving cooperation among hospitals [18].

Additionally, another interesting area of mobile application use is the collection and transmission of child birth data for vital statistical purposes. In Kenya a Nokia data gathering application was used to collect child birth data from the community and to send it to the ministry of home affairs for vital registration [19]. Similar applications have also been implemented by PLAN International in Thailand, Sri Lanka and Cambodia.

Opportunities for using Mobile Applications. The use of mobile phones in the HISs in developing countries has been observed to present opportunities in data transfer from remote communities and opening up communication channels between CHWs and their coordinators/supervisors in the districts [20]. Through these communications, mobile phones can be used for calling and sending text messages (SMS) for the purpose of supporting, supervising and giving CHWs feedback on their activities.

According to Chetterjee et al. [20] "*the extent of temporal mobility of the user will positively affect the use of a mobile device within the healthcare context.*" Contrary to the paper-based system where transfer of data and communication need a physical presence of both parties in a fixed location, users of mobile phones can transfer data and communicate in a timely manner from different places. It is therefore no surprise that Iluyemi and Briggs [21] indicate that supporting CHWs with mobile applications should be considered as a top priority in developing countries.

Regardless of these various mobile application implementations, there is, however, limited research on the use of mobile phone by CHWs for reporting birth information in the HIS. Thus our research aims to fill this gap as it explores the adoption of mobile applications to support and improve medical birth registration.

3 Research Methodology

In this study, qualitative research methodology was employed and data was collected using detailed interviews, document reviews and observations. These are presented in this section.

3.1 Interviews

Structured and unstructured interviews were conducted to six village health workers, seven traditional birth attendants, two health facility workers and three health managers from the district. Six village health workers interviewed were among the eleven in the Kwala ward. They were interviewed in groups of two to three using structured questions. Among twenty traditional birth attendants in the Kwala ward, seven were interviewed using one-to-one interview where the questions were open-ended. Interview sessions conducted to village health workers and traditional birth attendants were tape recorded at an average of thirty minutes each. Objectives of the interviews were to understand information they collected in the community regarding births, how and where it was reported and challenges they faced in collection, recording, transferring and storing the information.

Interview sessions conducted to health facility workers at the Kwala health center were one-to-one and open-ended questions were used. These health workers were the two personnel in-charge of the health center. The objective of interviewing this group was to get an understanding on how health facility workers worked together with CHWs (Village health workers and Traditional birth attendants) and how they supported CHWs in their daily activities.

Health managers, from Kibaha district were involved in one-to-one interview sessions which had open-ended questions. They were interviewed with the objective of understanding how they perceived, valued and supported the contribution of CHWs in reporting births taking place in the community. Another objective was to assess procedures used for providing feedback and supportive supervision.

3.2 Observations

Observations and participatory observations were conducted in this study. Participatory observations were done during training sessions, formal and informal discussions and meetings. The objective of the participatory observations was to acquire an understanding of how CHWs performed their activities and the challenges they faced. The other objective was to understand CHWs' perspectives on using a mobile phone application in reporting data they collected.

This research also participated in training conducted to CHWs by health managers from the district by engaging in several discussions. The training had the objective of improving CHWs' skills and knowledge on data collection, recording and storing. The training took eight days where twenty traditional birth attendants and eleven village health workers participated.

Several observations were made at the health center during Antenatal, Postnatal and children clinic sessions. The objective was to understand the practices of health workers in interviewing mothers, recording data while providing services and referring mothers and/or children to hospitals.

3.3 Document Reviews

To further improve the richness of data collected from the interviews and the observations, this study reviewed several documents. These included epidemiology reports, country demographic survey reports, Ministry of Health curriculums for training CHWs and data collection tools including different village registers.

4 Findings

This section presents findings on current practices in birth registration and the involvement of different stakeholders in data collection, recording, transferring and storing.

4.1 Stakeholders and Activities

This study identified five different stakeholders that were involved in communicating birth information directly and indirectly from the community level to the district. These were village health workers, traditional birth attendants, health facility workers (Nurse Midwife and MCH aid), district health managers (village health workers' coordinator and traditional birth attendants' coordinator) and village government. All the stakeholders were directly involved in the HIS except the village government. This paper presents findings on directly involved stakeholders. Table 1 shows activities of each stakeholder in communicating birth information from the community to the district level.

The main goal of traditional birth attendants in the HIS was to ensure that records were available when their coordinator from the district went to supervise them. They recorded individual-based data in standardised registers on deliveries including the name of the mother, father and village head, gender of the baby, condition of the baby and the mother if any, and reasons for death (Mother, Child) if any. Although traditional birth attendants could not read and write, they used village health workers or anyone close to them to write for them in the registers. Despite of all the information collected and recorded, six out of seven traditional birth attendants

Table 1. Activities Done by Each Stakeholder

Activity	Stakeholder			
	Traditional Birth Attendant	Village Health Worker	Health Facility Worker	District Health Manager
Data Collection	- Assist deliveries in their home or client's home	-Household visitations -Observations -Gather observations from traditional birth attendants	-Health center client visitations -Outreach Activities -Gather reports from village health workers	-Gather paper based reports from health facilities and traditional birth attendants
Data Recording	-Record data on Paper-based registers	-Record data on Notebooks	-Record data on Paper based registers, Report forms and Tally forms	-Enter data into District Health Information Software (DHIS)
Data Transfer	-Nowhere	-Present a quarterly report to health facility nurse in-charge	-Present quarterly reports to the district	-Manually and electronically through DHIS to the region
Data Storing	-in home cabinets	-Personal files at home	-File reports, tally forms and registers in cabinets	-Electronically in the DHIS database

indicated that no one had read nor supervised their data recording in their registers since they were given the registers in 2006. The recorded data was therefore not transferred anywhere.

Health managers as one of the stakeholders had to ensure that complete and accurate data was collected from traditional birth attendants and health facilities every quarter and entered into the DHIS. This research found out that collection of data from traditional birth attendants had never been done with the exception of one traditional birth attendant who could read and write, and whose work was supervised over mobile phone communications. Health managers worked with only aggregated data.

Village health workers were driven by two main goals. The first goal was the same as that of traditional birth attendants, to ensure the availability of records when they were supervised. The other goal was to present monthly and quarterly report on all births that took place in the community to the health facility nurse in-charge and the village government. Village health workers did not use standardised registers for data collection and reporting, they used notebooks. Data was recorded in individual-based format then it was aggregated every month and quarter for reporting. Unlike most of the traditional birth attendants who were aged women (40 – 80 years) and could not read, write and use mobile phones, village health workers could read, write, use a mobile phone and owned one. Furthermore, findings indicate that data reported by village health workers to the health facility was not incorporated in the health facility reports all the time. The nurse in-charge explained that sometimes the information was not complete. As a result this information remained in the village health workers' notebooks. Health facility workers also indicated that they provided support to village health workers on how to go about different observations. Most of this support was provided using their mobile phones.

Health facility workers who were medical professionals, worked in health centers and dispensaries collectively named health facilities. Their main goals were provision of health services, recording and reporting complete and accurate data timely. Reports were sent to the district and sometimes the district health managers picked up reports from health facilities. At the health facilities, data was collected and reported using standardised tools such as registers, tally forms and report forms.

4.2 Supportive Supervision and Feedback Provided to CHWs

This study also aimed to investigate how CHWs were motivated by health managers to improve their performance in the provision of health services, and in data collection, recording, storing and transferring, by looking at the provision of feedback and supportive supervision. According to the ministry of health and social welfare regulations, CHWs were supposed to be supervised by their coordinators from the district at least once every quarter. This supervision was meant to collect reports and ensure that they were accurate and complete, to distribute supplies (medical and stationary), to present reminders and announcements on mobilisation activities prevailing at that time and to ensure that everything was in order. However the supervisors did not have a checklist on what to supervise, they only checked what they remembered to check. Health managers also indicated to be constrained by budget allocated for supervision and many responsibilities which hindered them to provide regular supervision. One said,

"We only supervise them when there is a budget supporting that"

Due to the constrained budget and unmet needs of village health workers such as sufficient skills, adequate supply of stationeries (notebooks, forms, standardised registers, pens, calculator and folders), technical support on provision of services and sufficient means for transportation to all households; village health workers faced difficulties in data collection, recording, storing and transferring. One village health worker said,

"Households in my village are far from each other and others are very remote and I don't have a bicycle to use but I walk anyway to make sure I collect accurate data in all my households"

However this was not the case for traditional birth attendants, with the exception of one, because they operated as private providers. Nevertheless, the health managers at the district provided them with registers for recording data on delivery outcomes for the mother and the baby. The health manager who was the traditional birth attendant coordinator did not provide attention on the data recorded and supervision provided to traditional birth attendants was highly neglected.

As long as there were few or no supervisions and support provided to CHWs, there was also few feedback given. Village health worker indicated that they never received feedback on their performance in data they had collected and reported based on maternal health. They received feedback on other activities they performed for parallel programs. Traditional birth attendants indicated that the only feedback they received were warnings when they did something wrong. However one traditional birth attendant indicated that she was receiving feedback based on her performance in reporting of data and provision of services through her mobile phone.

5   Analysis

Analysis of the findings reveals that, at the community level, individual-based data was collected and recorded by village health workers and traditional birth attendants.

Village health workers recorded the data in notebooks and aggregated it at the end of the month and quarter and reported it upwards to the health facility where it was compiled in health facility's reports and further reported to the district. Data from traditional birth attendants, which was recorded on standardised registers, was reported to the district in individual-based format. However only one out of seven traditional birth attendants was reporting the collected data. Figure 2 presents a visualization of the sequence of activities in the flow of birth information among different health stakeholders from the community to the district level.

The diagram depicts a weak link (dotted arrows) in the flow of maternal health data from the community to the district level. Despite the fact that the data were not properly reported, they were recorded in traditional birth attendants' registers and village health workers' notebooks. The state of under-reporting was led by several practices among stakeholders in the HIS. These practices included a poor support structure as indicated in the findings that CHWs received unreliable support, supervision and feedback on their work performance from district health managers and health facility workers.

To improve the state of poor reporting, this study has perceived the use of mobile phones at the community level as an opportunity to bridge the gap in data flow in the HIS and to strengthen the weak support structure. Looking at the mobility nature of work of village health workers' activities and the capability of a mobile phone to support this as presented by Chetterjee et al. [20], this study proposes a mobile phone application infrastructure that could be implemented to support the work practices in the HIS. Figure 3 presents the envisioned mobile phone application infrastructure.

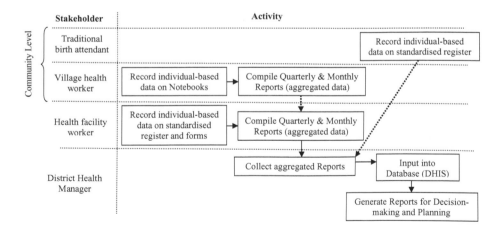

Fig. 2. Sequence of Activities in the flow of birth information from the community to the district level

With this infrastructure in place, the broken link in the flow of information as indicated in Fig. 2 between the community and the health facility levels would be bridged. Village health workers would be reporting data they recorded and data from

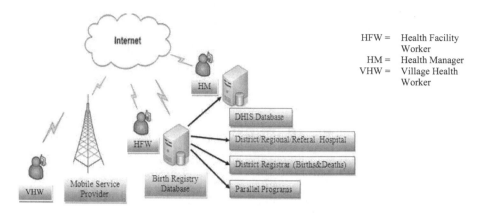

Fig. 3. Envisioned Mobile Phone Application Infrastructure

traditional birth attendants' registers to the health facility through the mobile application. This application would also present opportunities for health managers and health facility workers to support, supervise and present feedback to community health workers remotely, without travelling to meet them in remote areas as was done with one of the traditional birth attendants. This might promote desirable practices in collecting, recording, storing and transferring maternal health data in the HIS.

6   Discussion and Conclusion

This section presents the discussion based on the findings and theoretical reflections, and concluding remarks on answering the research questions.

6.1   Current Practices

As presented in the findings, current practices indicate lack of backward flow of information in the form of feedback with the exception of one traditional birth attendant whom health managers could communicate with through a mobile phone. Village health workers and traditional birth attendants were also provided with very little support and this went hand in hand with provision of little or no feedback. This situation has also been observed in other developing countries [8, 10] and it created reluctance in reporting and thus hindered the flow of information.

Desirable and Undesirable practices. This section presents current practices among stakeholders categorised as desirable and undesirable practices as presented in Table 2.

Table 2. Desirable and Undesirable Practices

	Stakeholder	Desirable Practice	Undesirable Practice
Data Collection	Village Health Worker	-Eager to go house to house to get complete and accurate data	-Remote households could not be reached on time
	Health Facility Worker	-Gathered reports from VHWs which contained community data	-No feedback provided to VHWs on the data gathered from their reports
	Health Manager	-Gathered reports from health facilities and traditional birth attendants	-Provided no transport mechanisms to VHWs for household visitations and reports presentation to the health facility -Irregular supervision provided to VHWs and TBAs on data collection -No collection of data from TBAs' registers
Data Recording	Village Health Worker	-Noted all observations possible -When they needed assistance they called the HFWs (using mobile phones and/or physically meet) for support	-When out of stationary data was recorded later sometimes the observations were forgotten -Using un-standardised register – VHWs recorded what they thought was necessary
	Health Manager	-Provided technical support to a TBA through a mobile phone	-Provided VHWs with inadequate stationeries for recording the collected data -Little/No supervision was provided to VHWs and TBAs on data recording -No checklist for provision of supervision -Provided negative feedback only
Data Transferring	Village Health Worker	-Ensured the completion of monthly and quarterly reports	-Late reporting to the Health facility
	Traditional Birth Attendant		-Not reporting the data recorded
	Health Facility Worker	-Ensured the completion of monthly and quarterly reports	
	Health Manager	-Provided feedback on reports to a TBA through a mobile phone	-Providing no transport means to VHWs to send reports to the health facility
Data Storing	Village Health Worker		-Not keeping reports for their own data utilisation or further reference
	Traditional Birth Attendant	-Stored their registers	
	Health Manager	-Stored data electronically where it was readily accessible and sharable	

Findings indicated that current practices which were undesirable among village health workers, traditional birth attendants, health facility workers and health managers in the HIS fuelled challenges in data collection, recording, transferring and storing. Undesirable practices also contributed in creating the gap in the flow of birth information from the community to the health facility and further to the district level. Furthermore, the weak support structure was often provoked by the way supportive supervision was conducted without having a checklist of what to supervise and low/no budget allocation for supervision, transportation and stationeries necessary for data recording, reporting and storing. Rowe et al. [6] indicate that, health managers need to understand these practices and this will give them an insight on which practices to enforce and which to abolish among health workers. In light of studies conducted in developing countries [7-11], motivation has been used to enforce desirable practices.

6.2 Adaptation of a Mobile Application

The communication gaps in communicating birth information in the HIS can be bridged by the use of mobile applications as the case in other studies in developing countries [16-21]. According to Chatterjee et al. [20] the adaptation of mobile applications can support communication because of the mobility characteristic of using devices such as mobile phones. The use of mobile phones has also been observed to be beneficial in resource constrained areas [22]. Despite the fact that CHWs are accustomed to work in a paper-based system (using paper, pencils, pens, erasers) [23], findings indicated opportunities in using mobile phones to improve communication in the HIS that would enhance provision of reliable and timely supportive supervision and meaningful feedback.

Support in Collection, Recording and Transferring of Information. Provision of support has been observed as one of the factors for motivating CHWs to improve their performance in many developing countries including Kenya, Benin, Vietnam and Mali [7-11]. Support also offers health workers a helping hand in the completion of their tasks by improving knowledge and skills in performing tasks which may lead to avoidance and/or reduction of mistakes [8, 9, 12]. Rowe et al. [6] further indicate that in most developing countries provision of supportive supervision to CHWs offers a connection link between the community and the rest of the formal HIS. Findings indicated the possibility of using mobile phones to provide support and supervision to CHWs who had mobile phones. If this practice could be formalised and improved, there would be improvements in accuracy and completeness of data collection and recording from the community. In this regard, a mobile phone could be adopted as a tool to strengthen the present weak support structure in the HIS and this would motivate CHWs to collect and report accurate and complete information [9].

Support also includes the provision of meaningful feedback to CHWs. Health managers and health facility workers could use mobile phones to send feedback to CHWs as a way of enforcing desirable practices. Provision of feedback also open doors for good communication between CHWs and their supervisors and this would motivate CHWs because it would create a feeling that their achievements are recognised [9] and appreciated [10].

Envisioned Mobile Application. This section presents the envisioned mobile application (as presented in Fig. 3) which will be implemented in a later stage of this research. Based on the current practices and the infrastructure in the HIS, this application is perceived to improve flow of birth information from the community to the district level by providing opportunities for fast and timely transfer of information and by creating communication channels between health managers, health facility workers and village health workers for provision of supportive supervision and meaningful feedback to provoke desirable practices in data collection, recording, storing and transferring.

For data collection and recording, mobile phones will be used by village health workers to record individual-based information on births collected in their notebooks and traditional birth attendants' registers and send it to a database (medical birth registry) placed at the health center through the internet. The data will be recorded in standardised registers on a mobile phone and every individual will be uniquely identified in the system. Upon the reception of the information, the database will automatically send a feedback (notification of receipt) through SMS. All the information sent to the medical birth registry will be approved by the health facility nurse in-charge before it is committed to the database. At this point the health facility nurse in-charge will use a mobile phone to call or send an SMS to the respective village health worker for further clarification if needed.

From the medical birth registry, the information will be compiled (aggregated) monthly and a report will be sent electronically to the DHIS database at the district. The aggregated reports will also be given (as a print out) to individual village health workers based on the data they reported to the health center in that particular month and/or quarter. At the district, the information will be approved by health manager and then saved into the DHIS database. At this point, the information will be readily available to be shared by different stakeholders such as district health workers, district and referral hospitals, district registrar of births and deaths for vital registration, and parallel programs.

The undesirable practice of late reporting of data collected by village health workers, as observed in the findings, will be eliminated because data will be transferred to the database right after recording it and there will be no need of manual preparation of monthly and/or quarterly reports. This will also reduce the transportation costs for transferring data from the community to the health facility.

Furthermore, in the envisioned system, the weak support structure in the HIS will be strengthened whereby instructive support on technical aspects in the provision MCH services which affects in one way or the other, data collection, recording, storing and transfer, will be provided to village health workers by health managers and health facility worker whenever needed through calling and/or sending SMS. Health managers and health facility workers will also be urged to provide meaningful (constructive) feedback after the completion of tasks and on the performance of village health workers and traditional birth attendants on monthly bases and whenever necessary. To facilitate supportive supervision, the mobile application will also provide health managers and health facility workers checklists to be used for providing regular supervision.

The envisioned use of mobile phones as a tool to facilitate communication of birth information between community health workers in the community, health facility workers in the health facilities and district health managers in the district, is perceived as a rewarding mechanism [24] which will promote desirable work practices in the HIS.

References

1. Walraven, G.E.L.: Primary reproductive health care in Tanzania. European Journal of Obstetrics & Gynecology and Reproductive Biology (69), 41–45 (1996)
2. WHO, World health report 2005. Making every mother and child count. Geneva (2005)
3. Bergsjø, P., et al.: A Medical Birth Registry at Kilimanjaro Christian Medical Centre East African. Journal of Public Heath 4(1), 1–4 (2004)
4. MHSW. Health Services System Structure 1993,
   http://www.moh.go.tz/health%20services.php (cited April 21, 2010)
5. Lippeveld, T.: Routine Health Information Systems: The Glue of a Unified Health System. In: Potomac. JSI, Washington DC (2001)
6. Rowe, A.K., et al.: How can we achieve and maintain high-quality performance of health workers in low-resource settings? Lancet 366, 1026–1035 (2005)

7. Henderson, L.N., Tulloch, J.: Incentives for retaining and motivating health workers in Pacific and Asian countries. Human Resources for Health 6(18) (2008)
8. Mathauer, I., Imhoff, I.: Health worker motivation in Africa: the role of non-financial incentives and human resource management tools. Human Resources for Health 4(24) (2006)
9. Franco, L.M., Bennett, S., Kanfer, R.: Health sector reform and public sector health worker motivation: a conceptual framework. Social Science and Medicine 54, 1255–1266 (2002)
10. Dieleman, M., et al.: Identifying factors for job motivation of rural health workers in North Viet Nam. Human Resources for Health 1(10) (2003)
11. Hongoro, C., Normand, C.: Health Workers: Building and Motivating the Workforce. In: Disease Control Priorities in Developing Countries. Oxford University Press, New York (2006)
12. Rahman, S.M., et al.: Factors affecting recruitment and retention of community health workers in a newborn care intervention in Bangladesh. Human Resources for Health 8(12) (2010)
13. VitalWaveConsulting, mHealth for Development: The Opportunity of Mobile Technology for Healthcare in the Developing World. UN Foundation-Vodafone Foundation Partnership, Washington, D.C. Berkshire, UK (2009)
14. Chatterjeea, S., et al.: Examining the success factors for mobile work in healthcare: A deductive study. Decision Support System 46(3), 620–633 (2009)
15. Kinkade, S., Verclas, K.: Wireless Technology for Social Change: Trends in Mobile Use by NGOs, in Access to Communication Publication Series. UN Foundation–Vodafone Group Foundation Partnership, Washington, DC and Berkshire, UK (2008)
16. UNICEF, Using Mobile Phones to Improve Child Nutrition Surveillance in Malawi (2009)
17. UN, Compendium of ICT Applications on Electronic Government. In: Department of Economic and Social Affairs (ed.) Mobile Applications and Learning, vol. 1, United Nations, New York (2007)
18. Dinis, M., et al.: Telemedicine as a Tool for Europe-Africa Cooperation: A Practical Experience. In: Villafiorita, A., Saint-Paul, R., Zorer, A. (eds.) AFRICOM 2009. LNICST, vol. 38, pp. 86–94. Springer, Heidelberg (2010)
19. Raftree, L.: Modernizing Birth Registration with Mobile Technology (June 28, 2009), http://lindaraftree.wordpress.com/2009/06/28/modernizing-birth-registration-with-mobile-technology/ (cited November 20, 2009)
20. Shrader-Frechette, K.: Ethics of Scientific Research. Rowman & Littlefield Publishers Inc. (1994)
21. Iluyemi, H., Briggs, J.: eHealth and Global Health: Investments Opportunities and Challenges for Industry in Developing Countries. In: Electronic Health Care First International Conference. Springer, London (2008)
22. Manda, T.D., Herstad, J.: Implementing Mobile Phone Solutions for Health in Resource Constrained Areas: Understanding the Opportunities and Challenges. In: Villafiorita, A., Saint-Paul, R., Zorer, A. (eds.) AFRICOM 2009. LNICST, vol. 38, pp. 95–104. Springer, Heidelberg (2010)
23. Johnsonl, W., et al.: Bridging the Paper and Electronic Worlds: The Paper User Interface. In: Human Factors in Computing Systems. Communications of the ACM, Amsterdam (1993)
24. Skinner, B.F.: Science and Human Behavior. MacMillan, New York (1953)

Utilization of ICTs in Multipurpose Community Telecentres in Rural Malawi

Patrick Albert Chikumba

Department of Computing and Information Technology,
The Polytechnic, University of Malawi
Private Bag 303, Chichiri, Blantyre 3, Malawi
patrick_chikumba@yahoo.com

Abstract. In order to empower rural communities the most important issue is an access which is the crucial factor to get to ICT tools for advancing social and economic developments. These technologies can create new types of economic activities, employment opportunities and enhance social interaction and networking among people. Access to basic telecommunications services is a basic right of the population of Malawi and telecommunications is one of the most important tools in reduction of poverty in rural areas. The government of Malawi established a pilot network of public access ICT facilities called Multipurpose Community Telecentres in rural areas with an aim of addressing the digital divide by providing universal access to basic ICT services in reasonable walking distances by establishing telecentres in strategically located positions. Pattern access and use of telecentre services varies across different socio-economic groups. It also depends on the service and the way its delivery is structured. Therefore, this paper discusses the utilisation of these ICTs in telecentres in rural areas in Malawi considering challenges and opportunities.

Keywords: Accessibility of telecentres, Facilities at telecentres, Telecentre, Telecentre services, Utilisation of ICTs.

1 Introduction

Information and Communication Technology (ICT) can be an extremely powerful enabler in efforts to bring positive and sustainable development to countries around the globe. A major gap has always existed between affluent people living in developed societies with access to modern information technology and underprivileged people living in impoverished and rural communities in underdeveloped countries. Even today, an unequal adoption of technology excludes many from harvesting the fruits of the digital economy. One major intervention to address the problem of literacy is through the use of ICTs. In order to empower rural communities the most important issue is access which is the crucial factor for them to get to ICT tools for advancing social and economic developments as these technologies can create new types of economic activities, employment opportunities and enhance social interaction and networking among people [7].

R. Popescu-Zeletin et al. (Eds.): AFRICOMM 2010, LNICST 64, pp. 93–101, 2011.
© Institute for Computer Sciences, Social Informatics and Telecommunications Engineering 2011

With the increasing use of ICT in daily live there is a great tendency for those in marginalised areas and groups to be left out in the online activities due to geographical limitation and limited ICT literacy level [7]. Access to information has the potential to bring about necessary social and economic changes in a society. Information evolution often results in greater socio-economic inequity in a society due to differential access to computers and Internet. The digital divide may be overcome in the long term by providing access to public information systems through telecentres.

Telecentres have hailed as the solution to development problems around the world because of their ability to provide desperately needed access to ICTs [3]. A significant number of such centres have been piloted and implemented by various governmental and development agencies in different countries [3][8]. Evidence of performance of telecentres in developing countries is still very limited and cases vary according to nature of location, year of development and regulatory environment, among others [3].

Access to basic telecommunications services is a basic right of the population of Malawi and telecommunications is one of the most important tools in a struggle to reduce poverty in rural areas [5]. A majority of rural communities in Malawi do not have access to any form of ICTs. Therefore, the government of Malawi, through Malawi Communications and Regulatory Authority (MACRA), and in partnerships with International Telecommunication Union (ITU), local and business communities established a pilot network of public access ICT facilities in rural areas in Malawi. These facilities are called Multipurpose Community Telecentres. The main aim is to address the digital divide by providing universal access to basic ICT services in reasonable walking distances by establishing telecentres in strategically located positions.

Currently, there are five telecentres which are operational and others are at development stage. The telecentre is a new concept in Malawi and it is at pilot stage. This paper discusses the utilisation of ICTs in Multipurpose Community Telecentres in rural areas in Malawi considering challenges and opportunities. Pattern access and use of telecentre services vary across different socio-economic groups such as class, occupation, caste, religion, education, age, gender, political and institutional affiliation. It also depends on the service and the way its delivery is structured.

2   Literature Review

According to Mukerji [6] telecentre is a generic term for all kinds of arrangement seeking to provide shared and mediated access to information and ICT-based services in rural areas through new technologies especially computers and Internet. A concept of shared access emerged as response to the perceived constraint that individual household in the rural area cannot afford such technologies. Access is mediated because a telecentre operator mediates between information, technology and people to overcome the barriers of low literacy, awareness about technology and availability of required skills.

The first telecentre in the world was set up in a village of 800 people of Sweden in 1985 [8] and its background was a great loss of population from rural communities in the northern part of the country. Especially younger generation was a big social concern in the region. Since then the idea has been spread to other countries in the world, including Malawi, with different reasons. For instance, in some countries like Malaysia, telecentres were introduced with the aim of (a) upgrading their rural community ICT literacy level; (b) providing access to the Internet; (c) increasing e-participation of communities in e-government, e-commerce and other online activities; and (d) empowering the rural communities socially and economically via the use of ICT [7].

Recent developments in ICTs are remarkable and bringing about great changes in the quality of life business [8]. There is also expectation that the benefits must reach rural and remote communities by application of these technologies. It has been recognised that diffusion of such new technologies is rather slow in rural sectors as compared with the urban courterparts. The telecentre concept has been piloted and implemented by both governments and communities as a new tool to introduce new ICTs to rural areas [3]. This can be especially useful in helping developing countries, like Malawi, take advantage of the information economy, accessing education, government information, healthcare and other services, and develop socially and economically.

Telecentres provide users with access to computers for word processing, games, CD-ROM usage, email and Internet. But the most popular services to date are the public phones, fax, printing, scanning, photocopying and binding, library, television and videos [4]. Degree of access to the telecentres differ from one telecentre to another due to several factors such as availability of technologies, economic status, issues of politics, training, information support, technical support and gender [4]. The most suitable telecentre, for example, considers (a) social and historical characteristics, pressing needs, cultural outlook, and level of education and literacy; (b) participatory mechanisms, political networking and interaction, and local power relationships; (c) assistance that the centre can offer to clients in terms of knowing and advising where to look for the information they need.

To be fully effective, a telecentre needs to become information and communication institution in its community. It is an innovation and thus a stranger to the community. Therefore, as suggested by different authors [1][2] it is very important to consider several conditions that include finances, society, politics, physical location, technology, local and relevant content, human resource and training.

It is important for the telecentre to have a long-term ability to generate enough income to meet operational and maintenance costs, in additional to a reasonable surplus for renewing broken and obsolete equipment. The main challenge is that much telecentres are introduced to generate sufficient income yet ensuring equal access for those who cannot afford to pay for access. Research and planning can reveal what telecentre services are feasible and affordable to the community members. Can the community pay for services? Is the community willing to pay for services?

Telecentres should be flexible, adaptive and most importantly creative in encouraging community members to participate. Social issues such as gender, age, and ethics should be well analysed and considered when establishing a telecentre. The telecentre is about looking beyond equitable access. The access must be something useful and this can be achieved through provision of local and relevant content which should be useful and user friendly. The most important reason for the failure of telecentres is their lack of suitable content [1][2].

Accessibility of a telecentre is also affected by its physical location. The telecentre should be located close to sites known by its community as stable institutions such as libraries, schools, and museums i.e. usual community meeting points [1][2]. It should be a place that encourages universal access by both men and women.

Implementation of ICT for development projects is a highly political process and ICT artifact needs to become institutionalized and accepted by these political actors [1][2]. Once the artifact is accepted as a social fact it is maintained because of its legitimacy regardless of the evidence of its technical value. Although the implementation of telecentres is political process, it is important the telecentre should be politically driven because it is for the community. Associating a telecentre with partisan organization such as a political party or religious groups runs the risk of excluding non-members of those groups.

3 Methodology

There are five operational telecentres in five different districts and only two were visited to collect data. One telecentre is the oldest (almost three years) and is run by the local community. It is located in remote area at a trading centre. Another one is a new centre which is less than half a year and is run by the business community. The main data source was semi-structured interviews supplemented by direct observations and reading. The semi-structured interviews was chosen because they give more "room" for interviewee (than structured interview) to provide his or her own point of view of the research subject. This type of interview also helped to maintain consistency for topics covered with each interviewee because a number of people were involved as participants from those two telecentres. A direct observation was mainly on users of telecentres. Participants (interviewees) were an official from MACRA, telecentre staff and users (clients). Five full days were allocated to each telecentre to collect data. Interviews and direct observations were conducted simultaneously.

4 Findings

Malawi has started implementing various rural projects including ICTs for sustainable rural development (ISRD) and ITU funded telecentre (ITU special initiative) projects. ISRD project was initiated by the Government of Malawi which proposed to introduce four pilot multi-purpose telecentres that will demonstrate the applicability of ICT tools to rural economic and social activities. Telecentres are run by local communities with the support from MACRA for a certain period of time. One of beneficiaries from this project is Thyolo-Goliati telecentre.

ITU special initiative project involves telecentres being implemented through the ITU funding and supervised by MACRA. Telecentres are operated fully by business communities. It has planned to implement seven such telecentres to be supervised by MACRA in seven districts and one of them is Balaka Tele-Business Centre. This project involves also implementation of six telecentres to be supervised by Malawi Postal Corporation (MPC) and they will be housed in existing postal buildings.

4.1 Thyolo-Goliati Telecentre

Thyolo-Goliati telecentre is the oldest. It was established in March 2007 and officially launched in January 2009 by the Ministry of Information and Civic Education. It is run by a local community (a chief as the chairperson and representatives of businesses, schools and hospitals) with the support from MACRA. It has five employees (three female and two male staff) who are paid by MACRA and they received training in computing skills.

Goliati is a trading centre in Thyolo district in the southern region of Malawi. It is about forty kilometers from Blantyre city. The telecentre is located at the trading centre surrounded by primary and secondary schools, market, shops and selling point of milk from local farmers. Access to Goliati is very easy because all roads to the centre are good throughout the year and public transport system is also available. The telecentre serves six villages.

Thyolo-Goliati telecentre offers the following services: telephone, Internet and email, secretarial (typing and printing), fax, photocopying, scanning and computer training. These services are offered on Monday through Friday from 7:30 am to 5:00 pm and on Saturday from 7:30 am to 2:00 pm, except the library which opens only on Monday, Wednesday and Friday from 9:00 am to 3:00 pm. Library service is not part of the telecentre. It is managed by volunteers from the local community with support from National Initiative for Civic Education (NICE).

Among these services, some are more in demanded than others. For instance, photocopying and library services are requested most followed by secretarial services, scanning, laminating and computer training. Telephone, fax and Internet are not demanded much. Binding service is not offered yet because there is no machine. Apart from telephone services, the telecentre also sells airtime for two mobile networks (Zain and TNM). For the Internet, the main challenge is connectivity. Previously there was a connection by a certain private company but no profits were made and now the centre is negotiating with Malawi Telecommunications Limited (MTL) to bring the connection. MTL is the biggest telecommunications company in Malawi and is currently offering fiber connection. The centre provides also computer training on request to teachers, students and farmers.

The services are offered to different people such as farmers, students and teachers. It was found that male users are visiting the telecentre more frequently than female counterparts. Many women are very shy to visit the centre and instead they ask their young ones to do on their behalf. The users are able and willing to pay for the services.

4.2 Balaka Tele-Business Centre

This is one of telecentres that are run by business community and supervised by the Balaka District Commissioner (DC). It was opened in April 2010 but not yet officially launched. This centre is sponsored by ITU and MACRA. It opens Monday to Saturday from 7:00 am to 7:00 pm and Sunday from 2:00 pm to 4:00 pm. It is managed by two directors, a manageress and an office assistant. The manageress and office assistant are paid by the telecentre from monthly income.

Balaka telecentre is located in a main bus terminal at Balaka trading centre. It offers services like binding, computer training, Internet, photocopying, secretarial and phone bureau. Lamination and library services are not yet offered. Among these services computer training, Internet, photocopying and secretarial services are highly demanded as compared to binding and phone bureau.

Computer training and Internet are highly demanded. Computer training is mainly offered to youth and the centre has designed a training program for various groups. The Internet users include youth (school students), business community, churches (particularly pastors) and passengers in transit at the bus terminal. Balaka Tele-Business centre fails to meet the demand of computer training and Internet services due to lack of computers. Currently there are only four computers for telecentre users and one for secretarial service.

Photocopying and secretarial services are also highly demand. Primary and secondary schools are main customers for these services particularly during examination periods. The centre is given the business of typing and photocopying of examination papers. Constraint is the photocopier when it is not in use due to lack of toner. For instance, when I was visiting this centre the photocopier had not been in use for about four weeks. The toner is not locally found. The photocopier was donated by ITU through MACRA and it is a new brand in Malawi and no servicing companies have accessories for this photocopier.

Male customers visit the centre more frequently than female counterparts. Main telecentre users include school students, teachers, pastors from different churches and people waiting for buses in the bus terminal. The users are able and willing to pay for the services.

4.3 Available Facilities at Telecentres

As shown in Table 1 below, it has been observed that telecentres have modern ICT facilities which need a good care. Comparing the two telecentres, it seems that the telecentres are in better position to take care of the ICT facilities. For instance, computers at Balaka telecentre have UPS and updated antivirus. On the another hand it is almost three years since Thyolo-Goliati was established but its facilities are still in good conditions. The question still remains: *Are these technologies well utilized at the telecentres? What are opportunities and challenges that these telecentres have?*

4.4 Most and Least Utilised Services at Telecentres

Some services at telecentres are more demanded than others and this differs from one telecentre to another and it depends on several factors. The most demanded services are secretarial, photocopying, Internet, email, computer training and library. Some services are not offered at a particular time because required facilities are not available or there is a technical fault or problem. Sometimes it is because of unavailability of accessories. This reduces utilisation rate of concerned services. For instance, library service is not available at Balaka telecentre but it is highly required by the community members especially school students and teachers and as observed at Thyolo-Goliati telecentre where the most affected service is Internet and email due

Table 1. Available facilities at the telecentres

No	Facility		Thyolo-Goliati		Balaka
1	Computers	-	4 HP Compaq dx2300 microtower & 2 Dell dimension E520/3100 with average of 80GB HDD, 1014 MB RAM, 1.80 GHz speed for HP & 3.00 GIIz for Dcll	-	5 Dell Vostro 200 with 240GB HDD, 1GB RAM and 2.53MHz speed
		-	No UPS	-	650 VA APC UPS on all machines
2	Software	-	Windows XP and Vista	-	Windows Vista
		-	An outdated antivirus	-	Updated antivirus on all machines
3	Printers	-	Canon LBP 5100 i-Sensys	-	HP Colour LaserJet CP1515n
		-	HP LaserJet 3050		
4	Fax Machines	-	Sharp FO-3150 laser facsimile	-	Canon i-sensys FAX –L140
		-	HP LaserJet 3050		
5	Copier	-	Canon iR 2016	-	Canon Laser Base MF6530
6	Laminator	-	Fuji Lamipacker Cubic	-	*Not available*
7	Phones	-	MTL Phones (Wireless)	-	MTL Phones (Wireless)
		-	HP LaserJet 3050		
8	Binder	-	*Not available*	-	CombBind C55
9	Paper cutter	-	*Not available*	-	REXEL SmartCut EasyBlade
10	Internet	-	*No connection*	-	Good and stable connection
11	Library	-	Books, Newspapers, Television and Radio	-	*Not available*
12	Scanner	-	HP LaserJet 3050	-	Canon Laser Base MF6530
13	Room	-	Large enough	-	Large enough
		-	Well air-conditioned	-	Well air-conditioned

to poor connection. This service is highly demanded at Goliati particularly by school students, teachers and other community members.

The least utilized services are scanning and binding at both telecentres. At Thyolo-Goliati telephones are in little demand and at Balaka telecentre the telephone is no longer requested for by telecentre users. It can be like this because of a fast growth of mobile phone usage by local community members. They have no need to move long distances to look for telephones to make calls. They use their mobiles to communicate with their relatives and friends. This can be evidenced at Thyolo-Goliati telecentre where it sells airtime units for mobile phones. The centre has realized that it can generate income from this business because most of its customers use mobile phones.

5 Opportunities and Challenges on Utilisation of ICTs

Government of Malawi (GoM) is very committed to the establishment of telecentres. It provides technical and financial support to a particular telecentre for a certain period of time until it finds out that the telecentre is able to sustain itself. For instance, since establishment of Thyolo-Goliati telecentre in 2007 GoM, through MACRA, has been paying salaries to the telecentre staff and also donated ICT equipment and it is responsible for maintenance. Even telecentres that are being run by business communities get some kind of support from MACRA. Balaka tele-business centre received ICT equipment and facilities from ITU through MACRA and MACRA is responsible for maintenance of these facilities for a year.

Even local communities are ready to manage these telecentres because they benefit from them such as employment as commented by the manageress of Thyolo-Goliati telecentre. All telecentre staff members are from within local communities and even some members are volunteers like in the library at Thyolo-Goliati telecentre. This means that there is a commitment from local communities which shows appreciation and ownership of these facilities.

Some organizations, local and international, give support to telecentres in Malawi. For instance, ITU provides support to some telecentres that are run by business communities and Malawi Telecommunications Limited (MTL) also provides support on Internet connections. Even Electricity Supply Commission of Malawi (ESCOM) is willing to assist telecentres in terms of power supply in the sense that sometimes telecentres negotiate with ESCOM not to switch off electricity due to a "load shading" in an area where a concerned telecentre is located especially when there are some functions that need electricity like the computer training.

There is also a high demand of telecentre services in rural communities which need the use of ICT tools. Primary and secondary schools, farmers, business community and individuals are willing to pay for the services because nowadays they do not travel long distance to get these services. For example, before the establishment of Thyolo-Goliati people were to travel to Blantyre (forty kilometers plus) for just photocopying and secretarial services.

Accessibility is also one of opportunities because telecentres are located to meeting points where people of all sorts of life come to conduct a variety of businesses. They are located close to schools, markets, bus terminals, shops, and so on which makes people not to travel long distances.

Telecentre staff members are equipped with necessary ICT skills that help them to handle the demand of services. They were trained how to use different ICT facilities. But it has been observed that they lack skills in basic computer diagnosis and minor maintenance. They always refer technical problems to MACRA and sometimes it takes time for the machine to be returned. Unavailability of facilities affects negatively their utilisation.

The telecentre staff members also require skills in finance management (particularly bookkeeping), marketing and office management. For instance, at Thyolo-Goliati telecentre computers are not well utilized because they fail to market computer training while their colleagues in Balaka have special computer training programs for school students and other individuals on weekly basis.

Another important challenge is the type of facilities and how locally they can be supported. It seems that in some cases donated equipment to telecentres is very new in Malawi and it is very difficult to maintain them in terms of accessories and technical expertise. At Balaka tele-business centre there is a copier whose toner is scarce in Malawi and even local copier dealers are failing to provide. It has been unusable for some weeks. It can be important to consider the local environment and identify ICT tools that can be easily maintained so that they benefit the local communities.

Some ICT facilities are no longer useful in telecentres due to fast growth of technology particularly cell phones (mobiles). Price of cell phones has gone down in Malawi which makes people even in rural areas to have them. This has affected the utilisation of phone bureaus at telecentres. Nowadays people do not value the phone bureaus and even fax facilities. They communicate with their friends and relatives through their mobiles and for sending documents they scan them and send as email attachments. They feel easier to use mobiles and Internet than phone bureau and fax.

6 Conclusion

Telecentres have provided universal access to basic ICT services in reasonable walking distances by establishing them in strategically located positions. Most required services are photocopying, scanning, computer training, Internet and email, secretarial services and library. It will be very useful to make sure each and every telecentre has got these services. Time between planning and implementation of telecentres is long which makes some services not to be useful as planned due to rapid growing of technology as observed in the phone bureau service. Needs analysis and revision of those needs are very important to conduct so that telecentres get ICT tools that will be fully utilized and at the end they benefit local communities.

References

1. Ali, M., Bailur, S.: The challenge of "sustainability" in ICT4D –Is Bricolage the answer? In: Proceedings of the 9th International Conference on Social Implications of Computers in Developing Countries, São Paulo, Brazil (May 2007)
2. Colle, R.D.: Memo to Telecenter Planners. The Electronic Journal in Information Systems in Developing Countries, EJISDC 21(1), 1–3 (2005)
3. Latchem, C., Walker, D.: Telecentres: Case studies and key issues. In: Perspectives on Distance Education, The Commonwealth of Learning, Vancouver (2001)
4. McConnel, S.: Telecentres Around the World: Issues to be Considered and Lessons Learned, ICT Development Group, CIDA's Canada-Thai Telecentre Project, Canada (2001)
5. Ministry of Information: Rural Telecommunications Policy: An Integral Part of the National Sector Policy Statement 1998, Government of Malawi, Malawi (2002)
6. Mukerji, D.C.: ICTs and development: A Study of Telecenters in Rural India. In: 10th International Conference on Social Implications of Computers in Developing Countries, Dubai, United Arab Emirates (2009)
7. Razak, N.A.: Empowering the Rural Communities Via the Telecentre. European Journal of Social Sciences 9(3) (2009)
8. Suzuki, A. and Chamala, S.: Role of Telecentres in Rural Development in Australia, Agricultural Information Technology in Asia and Oceania, The Asian Federation for Information Technology in Agriculture (1998)

Egypt Local Government Websites Maturity: Current Status

Hisham Abdelsalam[1], Hatem ElKadi[2], and Sara Gamal[1]

[1] Faculty of Computers and Information, Cairo University, 5 Ahmed Zewail St.,
Orman, Giza 12613, Egypt
h.abdelsalam@fci-cu.edu.eg
[2] Faculty of Engineering, Cairo University, Giza 12613, Egypt
hkadi@ad.gov.eg

Abstract. This paper investigates the maturity of Egyptian local e-government websites. The paper develops a model that fits a developing country context and is based on Quirk's Maturity Model and the Municipal e-Government Assessment Project (MeGAP) Model. The model is used to carry out a detailed content analysis of 22 governorates' web sites in Egypt. The results show a significant variability in websites' maturity in various spaces of the model. Information features have proved to be dominating, while features related to e-service and e-commerce are the least available on the local government websites.

Keywords: Egypt, local e-government, Quirk model, maturity, content analysis, MeGAP.

1 Introduction

Government bureaucracy is often held to be inefficient due to the lack of incentives to please its customers. Moreover, the potential customers, the citizens, have no alternative service provider available [1]. Electronic government or e-government has provided a means through which governments can improve citizen interaction with their government and at the same time change the traditional model of government [2]. In fact, the vital necessity of modernization and the introduction of enhanced business models that replace traditional ones have been realized by governments through e-government worldwide [3-4].

Technology allows governments to serve citizens in a timely, effective, and cost efficient way [1]. The key reasons for this public sector reform are to increase the efficiency of government operations, strengthen democracy, enhance transparency, and provide better and more versatile services to citizens and businesses [3, 5]. Local government, being closer to citizens and their interactions with the various levels of governments, is in a unique position to inform the public with the direction of future policy and to reflect the government's new vision and strategy. Like many other countries worldwide, the local e-government initiatives were set off in Egypt to improve the capabilities of enhancing service delivery to their citizens.

R. Popescu-Zeletin et al. (Eds.): AFRICOMM 2010, LNICST 64, pp. 102–112, 2011.
© Institute for Computer Sciences, Social Informatics and Telecommunications Engineering 2011

Broadly defined, e-government is the use of information and communication technology (ICT) to promote more efficient and effective government, facilitate more accessible government services, allow greater public access to information, and make government more accountable to citizens [6]. E-Government systems are becoming an essential element of modern public administration [7]. Assessing the effectiveness of these systems is becoming a necessity in order to ensure successful implementation [8].

This paper presents the results of a content analysis of 22 websites of Egyptian governorates. Following the introduction, the rest of this paper is organized as follows. Section 2 provides a brief introduction providing the context of Egypt e-government. The research methodology is presented in Section 3, followed by results in Section 4 and, finally, conclusions in Section 5.

2 Context

2.1 Egypt Local Government

The Arab Republic of Egypt (ARE or Egypt) lies in the south-eastern corner of the Mediterranean, mainly in Africa, with the Sinai Peninsula in Asia, separated by the Suez Canal. The majority of the country is desert across which the river Nile flows from the south to the Mediterranean in the north forming a Delta. Egypt has been a unified country for over five thousand years, mainly due to the river Nile.

Egypt area is 1 million square kilometers, with a population of around 78 million living on 5 % of the total area of Egypt. Ninety-seven percent of the population lives in the Nile valley with up to one-third of the population living in either Cairo or Alexandria. The United National Development Program (UNDP) has calculated that 46.8% of the economic and social establishments are in the governorates of these two cities, and that 23% of the labor force is in the same area. Most of the power is held by the central and not the local government.

Egypt is a unitary country that comprises of 29 administrative sections, called governorates (or municipalities), each of various sizes, populations, and resources. Governorates are administratively further divided into cities and districts which are, in turn, divided into smaller entities called neighborhoods in cities and villages in the districts.

The local entities have a certain degree of administrative freedom. Nevertheless, they are financially and politically managed by the central government. Local governments – represented in governorates – manage their operations based on rules, regulations and legal requirements created by the central government. However, they have autonomy in how they provide their service to citizens and how they manage their processes. Consequently, governorates might be organized in different ways. They have a degree of administrative autonomy, which when properly used can result in good administration, totally depending on the personality and abilities of the governor.

2.2 Egypt Local Government Development Program

Egypt has established its ICT strategy in 2001 in what has been known as the Egyptian Information Society Initiative (EISI). EISI was built on seven pillars; one of which was e-Government. This initiative was put into action and, hence, the e-government program in Egypt started in 2001. In 2004, program ownership was transferred to the Ministry of State for Administrative Development (MSAD), where the former e-Government Program Director (Dr. Ahmed Darwish) was appointed as the minister. This reflects the Egyptian understanding of e-Government as a natural component of administrative development and reform. Thus, the e-government program in Egypt became one of the two mandates of MSAD, the other one being the public administration institutional reform.

Initially, the e-government program consisted of four main subprograms among which came the Egyptian Local Government Development Program (ELGDP). In turn, ELGDP has three main projects: (1) service enhancement in municipalities which includes automation of services provided to citizens; (2) development of web portals for the governorates; and (3) citizen relationship management (CRM) systems.

3 Research Methodology

Many attempts have been made to establish models of e-Government maturity [9]; e.g. the United Nations [10] outlined a five stage model used to benchmark government web sites at a national level and other models have been presented in [11-13]. Local e-Government, however, needs to offer more than electronic replication of existing information and services as it provides an opportunity to offer new and enhanced services to the public, to increase the involvement of communities in policy making and improved service provision [9]. Some potential shortcomings in the stage models' capacity to capture the drivers and evolution of e-government [14] have derived alternative suggestions that appeared later [15-16] to show that governments mature in various spaces rather than in distinct linear stages.

This section presents the local e-government assessment methodology and its implementation procedure. The section starts by stating research questions and proceeds to detail different aspects of the methodology used.

3.1 Research Questions

The focus of this investigation was on two principal research questions: (1) What is a well suited model for assessing local government websites in the Egyptian context? (2) What is the status of local government websites in Egypt? To what extent have Egyptian governorates implemented more matured e-government services?

Most, if not all, available maturity models and assessment frameworks were designed and implemented in developed countries. The focus of the first research question will be on determining the applicability of two well developed models (Quirck's and MeGAP-3) in a developing country such as Egypt.

Being closer to citizens, local governments have the majority of interactions between government and the civil society. Their websites, thus, are expected to provide – effectively and efficiently – different service needed by their citizens. The second research question applies an assessment framework to examine how sophisticated (mature) these websites are in Egypt, providing insights that will help Egypt and similar countries improve the services provided via local e-government.

3.2 Model Used

Quirk's [15] model will be the corner stone of the research methodology of this paper. This model has been selected for this research as being of the widely accepted and used in the world [17], and because it emphasizes the disparate range of functions provided by local governments [18]. As the inappropriateness of a staged model approach to describe e-local Government was recognized in literature [16, 18], Quirck's model [15] uses the term 'spaces' to describe the maturity level approached rather than using a linearly ordered stages.

The original model uses five spaces. As outlined in [15], they are: (1) e-Management: improved management of people (2) e-Service: interface with customers, (3) e-Commerce: cash transactions (4) e-Decision-making: better informed public interest decisions and (5) e-Democracy: political dialogue citizen and community. Published work, however, merges the last two spaces into one (e.g. [17]). In this research, the original five spaces model will be used.

To assess the level of maturity of various governorates' websites on each of the five spaces, a content matrix was developed and used to examine the presence of a number of features. These features were extracted from three sources: (1) application of the model on Australian municipalities [18], (2) MeGap-3 [19], and (3) the authors (research team) of features of Egyptian municipal websites. This step extended the implementation framework presented in [18] by merging it with the MeGAP model. This research used the third version of the MeGAP (MeGAP-3) which has 68 distinct web performance dimensions (features). Features in MeGAP-3 that did not fit with the Egyptian context – e.g. pets' licenses – were excluded. The list of features is provided in Appendix A.

3.3 Scoring and Sampling

To evaluate the websites, each feature is given a score of: '1' if it is fully implemented; a reduced score of '0.5' if the feature is partly implemented; or '0' if the feature does not exist. Then, the score for each space equals the total scores of its features divided by the total number of features – in this specific space – and multiplied by 100 to give a percentage.

Assessment was made by a group of eight postgraduate students (evaluators) from Information Technology and Political Sciences majors. They received/attended two training sessions in order to effectively use the assessment model. For each governorate, assessment was conducted by each evaluator independently and then, results from different evaluators were compared and discussed in groups to reach a consensus upon scores. Out of the 29 governorates, 22 (76%) had a working website at the time of assessment (July 2010). Data was collected from a content analysis of the 22 governorates' websites. This sample represents 100% of available websites.

4 Results

This section presents the result of the assessment of local government websites. First, a comparison of the total scores is presented followed by the scores of different spaces, and finally the frequencies of most common and uncommon features.

4.1 Score Comparisons

We start with discussing the findings of the aggregated level; the 22 evaluated websites. Figure 1 presents the total score per governorate, and governorates are ranked in a descending order. As the figure shows, the scores range from 6 to 65 with an average of 38. Surprisingly, the capital city (Cairo) came third with 62.5 while the highest score was for Matrouh – a less developed governorate on the western borders of Egypt.

Another surprise was the score of the second capital of Egypt (Alexandria) which scored 36. It is noteworthy that Alexandria witnessed the first and most famous Egyptian e-government project that involved automating services in all of its councils. That project was referred to later on by e-Alexandria and became the role model for subsequent projects. Upper Egypt governorates – which are far less developed – achieved the lowest five scores. Such result was also expected due to the specific conservative nature of these governorates. It equally indicated the relatively low attention given by the central government for improving these governorates.

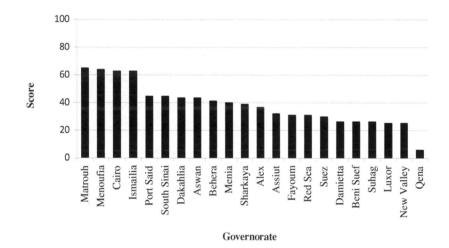

Fig. 1. Evaluation results by governorate total score ranked in a descending order

Figure 2 shows a comparison of scores of the 22 governorates with the population on the x-axis, which range from 150 thousands (South Sinai) to 7.8 million (Cairo) [20]. In line with [21], the figures depict an important point; "it is not necessarily the case that the most populous municipalities, and presumably those with the largest IT expenditures or the greatest need to offer services and functions to large and diverse populations, have the most extensive e-government solutions." As shown, the figures fail to prove the existence of a correlation between the population of a governorate and the sophistication of its website. Matrouh and Ismailia governorates have scored higher than governorates with much larger population such as Cairo and Alexandria.

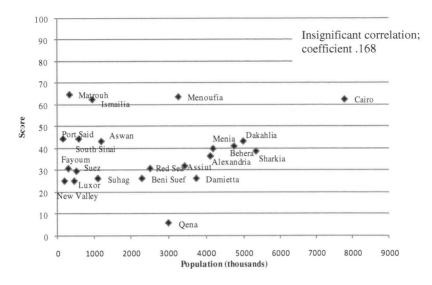

Fig. 2. Governorate total score *vs.* population

4.2 Spaces Comparison

Governorates' scores in each of the five spaces are shown in Fig. 3 through Fig 7. As expected, all websites scored in the e-management space (Fig. 3) are those intended to include features that assist citizens' navigation through the website. This space is also the first means to attract citizens to use governorate website rather than face-to-face or phone conversations. Out of the 22 governorates, 7 (32%) has a score more than 75% and 13 (59%) has a score more than 60%.

While all websites provide services, Fig. 4 shows a great deal of variability in scores with respect to the e-services space. Some provide only information about different services and necessary requirements and documents, while others provide downloadable forms and enable the citizen to obtain the service online. This space includes features which assist citizens to find information regarding different services provided by the local government. For the Egyptian context, this space has an increased importance as it provides information related to housing projects carried out by the government for low-income citizens and young families.

Scores of the third space, e-commerce, are shown in Fig. 5 revealing that only 41% of the websites have features related to e-commerce. This space covers the transaction handling involved in placing orders for services provided through the website. So, since the scores of the e-service space are already low, features related to order handling are not significantly present.

Figure.6 shows that a significant majority (95%) of websites have features belonging to the e-decision making space. The highest score, however, is 44%. This space provides information related to governorate operations on strategic and other managerial levels. Finally, the scores of e-democracy space are shown in Fig. 7. Surprisingly, a significant majority (73%) of websites have features belonging to this space and with average score higher than e-decision making space. Features that provide means to interact directly with the citizens seem to have a good deal of attention from the governorates.

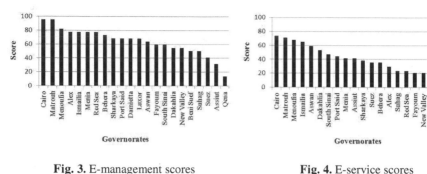

Fig. 3. E-management scores   Fig. 4. E-service scores

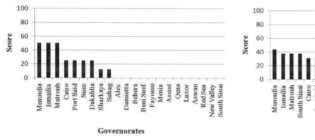

Fig. 5. E-commerce scores   Fig. 6. E-decision-making scores

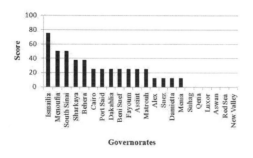

Fig. 7. E-democracy scores

4.3 Features' Frequencies among Governorates

Tables 1 and 2 partially list the different features and the number of governorates' websites supporting each feature. The percentage figures reflect a percentage of the total number of governorates. While Table 1 lists the most widespread features, which are supported by at least 60% of governorates' websites, Table 2 lists features found in few (0-30%) websites.

Table 1. Most Common Features

Feature	Space	N	%
Basic information	E management	22	100.0
Tourism	E Service	22	100.0
Website navigation	E management	21	95.5
Information for Businesses and investment	E Service	21	95.5
News and coming events	E management	20	90.9
Hierarchy	E management	19	86.4
Ownership of Content	E management	19	86.4
Contact details for the governorate	E management	18	81.8
Links to other organizations/businesses	E Decision making	18	81.8
Emergency Management	E management	17	77.3
GIS maps	E Service	15	68.2
Searchable Directory	E management	15	68.2
Sense of community	E Democracy	15	68.2
Job opportunities and training	E Service	14	63.6
Community information	E Decision making	14	63.6

Table 2. Most Uncommon Features

Feature	Space	N	%
FAQs	E Service	0	0
Online payments	E commerce	0	0
Email payment/ordering	E commerce	0	0
Economic indicators	E Decision making	0	0
Budget Report	E Decision making	0	0
Council minutes	E Democracy	1	4.5
Online support	E Service	2	9.1
Information Requests	E Service	2	9.1
Job application	E Service	3	13.6
Service tracking	E Service	4	18.2
Transaction handling	E commerce	5	22.7
Strategic Plan	E Decision making	6	27.3
Forums	E Democracy	6	27.3

Of the 15 features listed in Table 1, 11 features fall under the e-management space, 2 in the e-decision making space, 1 in each of the e-service and e-democracy spaces, and none falls under the e-commerce space. In other words, the most common functions concentrate on informing. However, e-service begins to penetrate the Egyptian community where tourism information and information for investment are among these features which reflect the attention given by local government to self revenue generation rather than solely depending on the national budget. As shown in Table 2, the bulk of e-service, e-commerce, and e-democracy features implemented totally fall under this table. This can be due to the belief that citizens would still prefer requesting local government services in person rather than online.

5 Conclusions

This paper investigates the maturity of Egyptian local e-government web sites through content analysis of 22 governorates' websites. The results show a variation in maturity levels of different governorates. Results reveal that Egyptian governorates' web sites are still in the first stage of maturity; cataloguing information [13]. This stage involves presenting information about government and its activities on the web available 24/7 to facilitate saving time and reducing cost. Most of the developing countries are still in this stage of maturity and have not reached yet the transaction stage which allows citizens to do their transactions with government electronically (i.e. citizens can pay taxes, fines, or fees). The paper, thus, suggests that more effort and attention must be given to improve local e-services provided through websites. Incentives should be given to move citizens from using physical face-to-face transactions to online services.

Acknowledgments. This work is part of the research project "Local e-Government in Egypt: Integrating Lessons into Planning," that was financed by a grant from the International Development Research Center (IDRC-Canada). The authors would also like to express their gratitude to H.E. Dr. Ahmed Darwish, Minister of State for Administrative Development for his support of the research team.

References

1. Kraemer, K.L., Dedrick, J.: Computing and public organizations. Journal of Public Administration Research and Theory 7(1), 89–112 (1997)
2. Lenk, K., Traunmuller, R.: Presentation at the IFIP WG 8.5, Working Conference on Advances in Electronic Government (February 2000)
3. Ho, A.T.: Reinventing local governments and the e-government initiative. Public Administration Review 62(4), 434–444 (2002)
4. Moon, M.J.: The evolution of e-government among municipalities: Rhetoric or reality? Public Administration Review 62(4), 424–433 (2002)
5. La Porte, T.M., Demchak, C.C., de Jong, M.: Democracy and Bureaucracy in the Age of the Web - Empirical Findings and Theoretical Speculations. Administration & Society 34(4), 411–446 (2002)
6. Traunmuller, R., Lenk, K.: Electronic government. In: Hameurlain, A., Cicchetti, R., Traunmüller, R. (eds.) DEXA 2002. LNCS, vol. 2453. Springer, Heidelberg (2002)
7. Torres, L., Pina, V., Acerete, B.: EGovernment developments on delivering public services among EU cities. Government Information Quarterly 22(2), 217–238 (2005)
8. Gupta, M.P., Jana, D.: EGovernment evaluation: A framework and case study. Government Information Quarterly 20(4), 365–387 (2003)
9. Shackleton, P., Dawson, L.: Doing it Tough: Factors impacting on local e-Government maturity. In: Proceedings of the 20th Bled eConference - eMergence: Merging and Emerging Technologies, Processes, and Institutions, Bled, Slovenia, June 4-6 (2007)
10. United Nations. Benchmarking E-government: A Global Perspective - Assessing the Progress of the UN Member States. United Nations Division for Public Economics and Public Administration, New York, United States (2002)

11. Baum, C.,Maio, A.D.: Gartner's four phases of e-Government model, Gartnert Group (2000), published in `http://www.gartner11.gartnerweb.com/public/static/hotc/00094235.htm`
12. Layne, K., Lee, J.: Developing fully functional E-Government: A four stage model. Government Information Quarterly 18(2), 122–136 (2001)
13. Reddick, C.G.: A Two-Stage Model of E-Government Growth: Theories and Empirical Evidence for U.S. Cities. Government Information Quarterly (21), 51–64 (2004)
14. Andersen, K.V., Henriksen, H.Z.: E-government maturity models: Extension of the Layne and Lee model. Government Information Quarterly 23, 236–248 (2006)
15. Quirk, B.: From Managing Change to Leading Transformation, Paper presented at the E-Government Summit, United Kingdom (December 2000)
16. Stamoulis, D., Gouscos, D., Georgiadis, P., Martakos, D.: Revisiting Public Information Management for Effective E-government Services. Information Management & Computer Security 9(4), 146–153 (2001)
17. Nawaz, M., Issa, M., Hyder, S.I.: e-Government Services Maturity Models. In: Proceedings of the 2007 Computer Science and IT Education Conference (CSITEd), The Republic of Mauritius, November 16-18, pp. 511–519 (2007)
18. Shackleton, P., Fisher, J., Dawson, L.: Evolution of Local Government EServices: the applicability of e-Business maturity models. In: Proceedings of the 37th Hawaii International Conference on System Sciences (HICCS 2004) (2004)
19. Public Sphere Information Group, The Municipality eGovernment Assessment Project (MeGAP), `http://www.psigroup.biz/megap/` (accessed June 2010)
20. Institute of National Planning. Egypt Human Development Report, Cairo, Egypt (2008)
21. Flak, L.S., Olsen, D.H., Wolcott, P.: Local E-Government in Norway: Current Status and Emerging Issues. Scandinavian Journal of Information Systems 17(2), 41–84 (2005)

Appendix A: Model Features

No.	Space	Features	Q	M	R
01	E-	Basic information	√		
02	Management	Web site navigation	√		
03		Contact details for the governorate	√		
04		News and coming events	√		
05		Hierarchy			√
06		Ownership of Content		√	
07		New features in the website			√
08		Searchable Directory		√	
09		Directions to Offices/Facilities		√	
10		Emergency Management		√	
11		Multiple languages		√	
12	E-Service	Service details	√		
13		GIS maps		√	
14		Transportation Schedule		√	
15		Education		√	
16		Information for Businesses and investment			√
17		Tourism			√
18		Service support/tracking	√		
19		FAQs	√		
20		Online support	√		
21		Tenders and auctions			
22		Information Requests		√	
23		Housing		√	
24		Building Permit Process		√	
25		Business License		√	
26		Vital Records		√	
27		Job application		√	
28		Job opportunities and training			√
29	E-Commerce	Transaction handling	√		
30		Online payments	√		
31		Ordering facility	√	√	
32		Email payment/ordering	√		
33	E-Decision-	Community information	√		
34	making	Links to other organizations/businesses	√		
35		Bulletin boards	√		
36		Economic indicators		√	
37		Budget Report		√	
38		Strategic Plan		√	
39		Streaming Audio of Meetings & Hearings		√	
40		Streaming Video of Meetings/Hearings		√	
41	E-Democracy	Sense of community	√	√	
42		Forums		√	
43		Scheduled E-meetings		√	
44		Council minutes	√		

Source Legend   **Q:** Quirck's [15, 18]   **M:** MeGAP-3 [19]   **R:** Authors (Research Team)

Student Performance in Computer Studies in Secondary Schools in Malawi

Patrick Albert Chikumba

Department of Computing and Information Technology,
The Polytechnic, University of Malawi
Private Bag 303, Chichiri, Blantyre 3, Malawi
patrick_chikumba@yahoo.com

Abstract. Malawi has a national policy for ICT which emphasizes introduction of computer lessons in the education, especially primary and secondary levels. In response to this, in five years ago, Government of Malawi through Ministry of Education introduced Computer Studies as an optional subject at senior secondary level. Since introduction of Computer Studies in secondary schools, there has been no literature on how students perform in this subject with emphasis on 'type' of secondary school, gender and school location. This paper highlights performance of students in Computer Studies with an aim of finding out which schools are doing better than others which will prompt for further study to investigate reasons of success or failure. Private secondary schools are performing better in Computer Studies than government secondary schools and this is not due to location, gender and 'type' of school. Particularly government secondary schools need to invest much more in computers, teaching materials and staff in order to delivery this subject to more students than it is now.

Keywords: Challenges in computer education, computer studies, ICTs in education, Malawi education system.

1 Introduction

Considered as a powerful tool to promote social and economic development, education has become a primary focus of the recently forged ICT for Development (ICTD) community, especially in the least developed countries. Introducing ICT as a tool to support the education sector has initiated substantial discussions since late 1990s [7]. Even in Africa, the point that socio-economic development will need to embrace the use of ICT appears to be widely recognised by governments and this is evidenced by a number of countries that have a national policy for ICT in place or under development [3].

Malawi has a national policy for ICT [4] which is under development and among other areas it points out the utilisation of ICTs in Education. It partly reads *"...The Government shall facilitate the development of the educational sector by introducing ICTs to all levels of the education as a key step toward the realization of the policy objectives. ..."* The policy emphasizes, among others, the introduction of computer lessons in the education, especially primary and secondary levels and using ICTs to

R. Popescu-Zeletin et al. (Eds.): AFRICOMM 2010, LNICST 64, pp. 113–121, 2011.
© Institute for Computer Sciences, Social Informatics and Telecommunications Engineering 2011

modernize the educational system in order to improve and extend access to educational, training and research resources and facilities.

In response to this, in five years ago, the Government of Malawi (GoM) through the Ministry of Education (MoE) in partnerships with British Council, SchoolNet Malawi and other stakeholders, introduced Computer Studies as an optional subject at senior secondary level (Forms 3 and 4). SchoolNet Malawi sources second-hand computers from various agencies which are then refurbished and distributed to Malawian schools. It also conducts training programmes for both teachers and students after each successful distribution phase although in most cases this training is not conducted as it is supposed to.

Education system in Malawi follows 8-4-4 pattern comprising primary, secondary and tertiary. Secondary education begins after eight years primary education cycle and consists of junior and senior cycles. Successful completion of the final two years of secondary education (senior cycles) qualifies eligible students to sit for Malawi School Certificate of Education (MSCE) examinations managed by Malawi National Examinations Board (MANEB) and Computer Studies is one of the subjects. Computer Studies mainly covers areas of basic computer hardware and software, word processing, spreadsheet, databases, PowerPoint presentation and network and Internet. Assessment is in point-scale of 1 to 9 as in any other subjects and the points are translated as follows: (a) DISTINCTION (1 and 2 points), (b) CREDIT (3, 4, 5, and 6 points), (c) PASS (7 and 8 points), and FAIL (9 points).

Since introduction of Computer Studies in secondary schools, there has been no literature on how students perform in this subject with emphasis on 'type' of secondary school, gender and school location. In this paper, 'type' of secondary school is in two dimensions: (a) whether a school is owned by the government or private organization/individual; or (b) whether a school enrolls only boys, only girls or both. This paper highlights performance of students in Computer Studies at MSCE with an aim of finding out which schools are doing better than others which will prompt for further study to investigate reasons of success or failure. Can 'type' of school, gender and location play a great role in performance of students in Computer Studies in secondary schools in Malawi?

2   Challenges in Computer Education

ICTs are used to help unlock the door to education and have opened up new potential. They facilitate administration of education and training, provision of learning content, and communication between learners and between learners and teachers. Computer-enhanced delivery of education and training is becoming increasingly widespread and can make education and training available to many more people around the world.

While there is an agreement that ICT can be a powerful tool for advancing education efforts going forward, the main challenge being faced today is turning the potential of ICT for Education (ICTE) into reality with results. This is a tremendous challenge, compounded by realistic fears that if not used properly, ICT can increase existing social and economic inequalities, particularly if access and use of ICTE is not equally available to everyone. With an active and transformative education policy and a supportive infrastructure, the development of a knowledge-based population can apply itself to sustained and equitable growth. ICT can play a vital role in increasing access to education as well as providing better quality education.

Since the world is now in information technology age, there is a need to keep abreast of time. One way achieving this is through the introduction of computer education in training institutions including secondary schools. Computer education is the ability to make the generality of the people computer literate which means ability to understand and operate computers [1]. For a country to be internationally competitive it is essential that its labour force is able to utilise and harness the advantages of ICTs. However, if tomorrow's leaders (the youth) are not able to fully utilise the benefits of ICT, as a result its population will be poorer.

Countries everywhere are facing similar challenges in implementing ICT in their education systems. The challenges of computer education are both educational and administrative. Where attempts are made to purchase computers for instructional purposes the costs of installation, maintenance and replacement are unavoidable

Some key challenges in integrating ICTs in education include implications of ICT-enhanced education for educational policy and planning, capacity building, language and content, financing the cost of ICT use, and infrastructure-related challenges [2][5][6]. Attempts to enhance and reform education through ICTs require clear and specific objectives, guidelines and time-based targets, the mobilisation of required resources, and the political commitment at all levels to see the initiative through. Availability of electricity and appropriate rooms or buildings to house the technology should be considered. Various competencies (for example in teachers, education administrators, technical support specialists and content developers) must be developed through the educational system for ICT integration to be successful.

According to Crawford [2] and Salim [6] as compared to other subjects barriers to providing computer education include: (a) study of ICT requires access to more expensive hardware, software and communication technologies; (b) technology changes rapidly and often unpredictably which results that schools must re-equip themselves much frequently; (c) there is insufficient hardware in many schools for students to have access whenever they need it, and they may have to share computers; (d) many teachers of ICT lack qualifications in ICT or computing, particularly at degree level or above, and very few have been specifically trained to teach ICT; (e) teachers of ICT must regularly learn new concepts, and re-learn old skills in new contexts, as the tasks that can be accomplished using ICT are extended; and (f) students may have more extensive ICT skills than their teachers as they often have access to more modern computer equipment at home and teachers generally rely on older equipment at school. Some of the above difficulties are due to schools' lack of staff with expertise in teaching and managing ICT in secondary schools, and more effective training, planning and resource management would be likely to lead to improvements.

3 Methodology

Examination results of Computer Studies of 2007, 2008 and 2009 academic years were used to find out the performance of students in this subject. Sample of schools was drawn from the list of examination centres (schools) whose ten or more students wrote Computer Studies examinations in each of those three years. Analysis was based on grade (distinction, credit, pass and fail), type of school, gender and academic year. Point 1 & 2 were considered as a distinction, point 3 – 6 as a credit, point 7 – 8 as a pass and point 9 as a failure. Absentees were also included in the analysis. The data was in Ms Access 2003 and results of Computer Studies were extracted into Ms Excel 2003 for the analysis that included summation, percentages and categorization.

4 Findings

4.1 School and Student Population

In Malawi, secondary school education is offered mainly through five types of schools namely (a) conventional secondary schools, (b) community day secondary schools, (c) open (distance) schools, (d) grant aided secondary schools, and (e) private secondary schools. Both conventional and community day secondary schools are fully run by the government. Open secondary schools are also run by the government through Malawi College of Distance Education while grant aided secondary schools get support from the government but are run by independent boards. Private secondary schools are run by individuals or private institutions. Some of these schools enroll boys only or girls only and others enroll both boys and girls.

Table 1. Sample Schools and Student Population

Year	Sample Schools	Students from sample schools written Computer Studies examination		
		Total	Male Students	Female Students
2007	77 out of 901	2461	1470	991
2008	97 out of 922	3186	1847	1339
2009	107 out of 944	3264	1870	1394

Note:

- Sample school has at least ten students wrote the Computer Studies examination in that year

It has been observed that number of schools interested to offer Computer Studies increased from 2007 to 2009 academic years (see Table 1) with also an increment in number of students but male students were dominating female students in all years. The increment was bigger from 2007 to 2008 than from 2008 to 2009 academic years. For example from the sample schools, in 2008 additions of 725 students wrote the Computer Studies examination while in 2009 there were only additions of 78 students. But there was no big difference between increment in male and female students.

In most of schools very few students registered to take this examination. In 2007 academic year out of 77 sample schools only 15 schools had 30% or more of students sitting for Computer Studies examination. The number increased to 20 out of 97 schools in 2008 and in 2009 the number dropped to 14 out of 107 schools.

4.2 Student Performance

Generally student performance was good in 2007 which dropped in 2008 and then improved in 2009 (see Table 2). In 2007 there was good number of students got distinction and credit but in 2008 there was big increase in failures and absentees which made distinction and credit to drop. For instance, distinction dropped from 11.1% in 2007 down to 1.4% in 2008. The student performance improved very much in 2009 especially in failures and absentees. Number of failures decreased from 24.0% in 2008 down to 10.6% in 2009.

Table 2. General Student Performance from the sample schools

Year	Distinction	%	Credit	%	Pass	%	Fail	%	Absentees	%
2007	273	11.1	819	33.3	694	28.2	286	11.6	389	15.8
2008	45	1.4	697	21.9	1128	35.4	764	24.0	552	17.3
2009	162	5.0	1110	34.0	1228	37.6	345	10.6	419	12.8

The male students did better than female counterparts in all three academic years. As shown in Table 3, male students who got distinction were twice as much as female students particularly in 2007 and 2009 academic years. Female students failed badly as compared to their male students. Both groups performed badly in 2008.

Table 3. Male and Female Student Performance in Percentages

Year	Distinction (%)		Credit %		Pass %		Fail (%)		Absentees (%)	
	M	F	M	F	M	F	M	F	M	F
2007	13.6	7.4	33.6	32.8	27.8	28.9	9.4	14.9	15.6	16.0
2008	1.6	1.2	22.9	20.5	35.9	34.7	21.3	27.6	18.3	16.0
2009	6.4	3.1	37.3	29.6	34.9	41.3	8.6	13.3	12.9	12.8

4.3 Good Performing Schools

Thirty-three schools were identified whose students sitting for Computer Studies examination in at least one academic year was 30% or more. Among these schools only 5 schools were good performing ones in all three years and they are boy's secondary schools except one school (Bambino private secondary school) and all run by private institutions. As indicated in Figure 1, performance of students was good. Majority were getting distinction and credit. Particularly Marist secondary school which had no student got a pass or failed the examination. Over 85% of students from Bedir and Marist secondary schools registered for Computer Studies examination in each academic year.

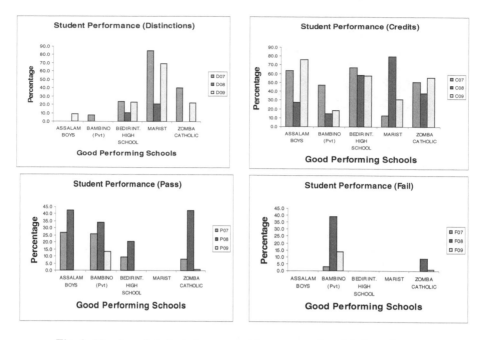

Fig. 1. Number of students (represented in percentage) and their performance

Apart from these good performing schools, some schools have started registering more students in Computer Studies mainly in 2009 academic year. There were eight secondary schools that registered between 30% and 49% of their students to sit for the examination in 2009 but student performance was worse than that of the good performing schools explained above. These schools are also run by private organizations. A majority of students got a pass except one school (Marymount secondary school) whose 10 students got distinction, 44 students got credit and only 5 students got pass. Two schools produced many failures and absentees. Out of these 8 schools two are girl's secondary schools and the rest enroll both boys and girls.

5 Why Such Performance in Computer Studies

There are several factors that can affect the performance of students in any subject at secondary schools in Malawi. For a student to perform well in examinations, he/she requires teaching and learning materials, well-trained teachers, good policies and planning and even dedication or commitment of students. In case of Computer Studies at secondary schools, every school needs, among others, a modern computer laboratory with adequate computers and Internet connectivity, qualified teachers, computer textbooks, financial support on computer operations and maintenance, and technical expertise.

The results have shown that schools run by private institutions or organizations are doing better in Computer Studies than those run by the government. Why is it so? Is it due to availability of adequate resources? Is it because they enroll only boys or only girls? Is it because they are located in cities or towns?

It can be said that private schools have better resources than government schools although there is no such evidence to support this in Malawi. Government employs teachers who are qualified and have gone through teachers training particularly University of Malawi (UNIMA). Unfortunately, when Computer Studies was being introduced UNIMA had no any degree program to train computer teachers. Even today, there are very few university graduates who have been trained as computer teachers. Most of the teachers of computer studies in government secondary schools went for short-time trainings in basic computing just to prepare them for starting off of the subject. The government is doing its best to support ICT in education by allowing universities in Malawi to introduce new degree programmes in computing for secondary school teachers. For example, UNIMA has introduced a degree in education majoring Mathematics or Statistics and Computing and it is also planning to introduce another degree in Business and Computer Studies education.

The government secondary schools depend much on donations for their computer laboratories and other equipment. Even maintenance and replacement of computers and peripherals are done by donating communities. In Malawi, SchoolNet Malawi plays a recommendable role in supporting government secondary schools by donating computers, providing training and also maintaining computers but the main problem is the capacity building because most of workers at SchoolNet are volunteers. SchoolNet Malawi cannot afford to support adequately all government secondary schools due to some constraints such as lack finances, difficult accessibility of schools, lack of personnel or computer experts and other logistics issues.

Sometimes failure is very high in government secondary schools because a good number of candidates sitting for Computer Studies and other subjects are 'external' who study on their own or through distance education. They do not receive adequate support from secondary school teachers. Sometimes they just register for Computer Studies examination and then decide not to write. This increases the number of absentees. For instance in 2008 academic year there were a lot of failures and absentees. It can be believed that more students registered for Computer Studies examination because they thought that this subject is simple after finding out that in previous year, 2007, the majority of candidates performed well. This can be evidenced in 2009 when there was very little increment in student registration.

As compared to government secondary schools, private secondary schools are doing well because they have resources such as teachers and computers. Private secondary schools employ teachers in the same way as the government does but for Computer Studies they employ computer experts to be teachers since teachers training institutions are not ready to provide adequate computer teachers. Some private schools provide training to those teachers on how to teach. Graduates in computing from universities can be employed as teachers of Computer Studies. It can be said that this contributes positive results in the subject.

At most of private schools all students sitting for Computer Students are 'internal' particularly the good performing schools mentioned above. These schools do not allow students learning somewhere to come and write examinations. This is just a policy of these schools with the aim of maintaining quality in order to survive in the school business. This helps the school management to assess the performance of their students and at the same time to make sure that available resources are utilized by their own students and nobody else.

Private secondary schools invest a lot on computers and other equipment so that students can get necessary theoretical and practical computing skills. They manage the equipment themselves. Since they invest a lot they need to take care of the computers in order to utilize them for maximizing profits.

Private school education is becoming very profitable business in Malawi and even Ministry of Education is monitoring and evaluating private schools very closely to make sure that education quality is maintained. The only way to be in school business is to produce good results at the end of year. Therefore there is a possibility that this prompts majority of private schools to use examination-oriented teaching style in which teachers teach 'examination', i.e. their target is on examination and not much on knowledge and skills. This also contributes to good results in Computer.

Type of school, location and gender do not contribute much to performance of students in Computer Studies. Although in early years boys secondary schools were doing better than other schools, it has been observed that girls secondary schools, such as Marymount and Providence have started to perform well and even schools which enroll both boys and girls are also performing well. Private schools that are doing well are boarding schools and their students come from different parts of the country with various academic and technological backgrounds. Some of these schools are in cities and towns while others are in remote areas like Marist secondary school but it is the best school in Computer Studies so far.

6 Conclusion

Private secondary schools are performing better in Computer Studies than government secondary schools and this is not due to location, gender and type of school. There is a possibility that it is because private schools have more adequate resources than their counterparts. It has been observed that more and more secondary schools and students are interested in Computer Studies and this shows that Malawi is in right direction in campaigning for ICT in Education. Secondary schools, particularly government secondary schools, need to invest much in computers and teaching staff in order to delivery this subject to more students than it is now. For Malawi to do well in ICTs it is necessary to make sure that each and every student attending secondary school education is taking this subject so that he or she can survive in the technological era.

References

1. Bada, T., Adewole, A., Olalekan, O.: Uses of computer and its relevance to teaching and learning in Nigerian educational system. Educational Research and Review 4(10), 443–447 (2009)
2. Crawford, R.: Teaching and learning IT in secondary schools: towards a new pedagogy? Education and Information Technologies 4, 49–63 (1999)
3. Farrell, G., Isaacs, S.: Survey of ICT and Education in Africa: A Summary Report, Based on 53 Country Surveys. infoDev / World Bank, Washington, DC (2007)

4. Malawi Government.: Malawi Information and Communication Technology (ICT) Policy, Government of Malawi (2003)
5. Mfum-Mensah, O.: Computers in Ghanaian Secondary Schools: Where does equality come in? Current Issues in Comparative Education, Teachers College, Columbia University (2003)
6. Salim, R.: Computer education at secondary school level, The Amader Gram Information Technology for Development (ICT4D) project (2007)
7. Stienen, J.: ICTs for Education: Impact and lessons learned from IICD-supported activities. IICD, The Netherlands (2007)

Enabling Business Intelligence Functions over a Loosely Coupled Environment

Giampaolo Armellin[1], Leandro Paulo Bogoni[1,2], Annamaria Chiasera[1,2],
Tefo James Toai[1], and Gianpaolo Zanella[1]

[1] GPI SpA, Via Ragazzi del '99, 13 - Trento, Italy
[2] Information Engineering and Computer Science Department - University of Trento,
Trento, Italy
bogoni@disi.unitn.it,
{garmellin,achiasera,ttoai,gzanella}@gpi.it

Abstract. Planning effective and well targeted actions to manage and improve
the local and national healthcare services requires institutions to understand and
analyse the real needs of the population based on reliable and timely statistical
analysis on citizens' health state. This is particularly important in developing
countries in which healthcare facilities lack ICT infrastructures and network
connectivity, making data collection and analysis particularly difficult with a
considerable manual effort leading to potentially unreliable or incoherent
information. In this scenario, we propose a generic communication
infrastructure, developed in the SIS-H project for Mozambique hospitals to
capture, communicate and analyse clinical events. Our solution enables the
exchange of data amongst healthcare facilities over all the different aggregation
levels of the hierarchical healthcare system of Mozambique regardless of the
availability of communication media (e.g., compact disk, usb stick, web-
internet). The plugin-based solution adopted supports reporting and Business
Intelligence analysis for exploring data at different granularity levels.

Keywords: Business Intelligence, e-Governance, plugin-based architecture.

1 Introduction

Improving accessibility and quality of health services is one of the outcomes of the
Mozambican Health Sector Strategic Plan (PESS 2007-2012 6, 5). Despite public and
external founds, medical assistance is not accessible to all the population owing to the
difficulty in coordinating and controlling the actions performed and a chronicle
deficiency of human resources. The World Health Organization points out the need of
monitoring systems to control resource flows, progresses and outcomes finalized to
monitor and evaluate health services [5], [9]. In the Strategic Plan for the Health
Sector [6] the role of such monitoring system is essential for decision makers to
manage and supervise the maintenance of hospitals. Another pre-requisite to evaluate
and improve health quality is to encourage community participation with the active
communication of the results of the analysis promoting transparency and
accountability.

R. Popescu-Zeletin et al. (Eds.): AFRICOMM 2010, LNICST 64, pp. 122–131, 2011.
© Institute for Computer Sciences, Social Informatics and Telecommunications Engineering 2011

In this paper we will report our experience in the development of a communication infrastructure applicable at the national level for the monitoring of the quality of healthcare system in Mozambique. We propose a lightweight and robust infrastructure that requires minimum resources to operate with poor or no connectivity to support people in the collection, processing and communication of statistical information with a simple and intuitive tool usable even by not trained personnel.

1.1 The Context

The structure of the Mozambican Healthcare System is level-oriented and hierarchical – i.e. operational units and hospitals are grouped according to managed services and geographical areas. The central hospitals of Beira and Maputo are at the top levels of the hierarchy (level IV hospitals) and refer directly to the ministry of health. Pemba provincial hospital is at level III and refers to the Provincial Health Office.

The ministry of health and the provinces provide economical support to operational units and hospitals and plan actions and projects to prevent and deal with chronicle and highly contagious diseases (like Malaria, HIV/AIDS, Cholera). These activities include, among others, economical investments to improve the infrastructures (hospitals' facilities like emergency rooms, intensive units, infective divisions), staff training, and education of the population for prevention.

Governing bodies need to know which are the real needs of the population to identify and deal with sanitary emergency, to plan an effective set of activities (e.g. the continuous and periodic surveillance required by HIV epidemic [7]) and to reduce waste of resources (staff and financial). In [10] it is highlighted how this requires at first the surveillance of the morbidity and mortality causes. The analysis of such statistical data allows on one side to understand the health state of the population and on the other side to monitor hospital resource utilization and in particular costs of hospitalization and staff employed. Based on these analyses the ministry of health can better plan public health interventions, for example to grant a suitable number of beds in hospitals or health posts facing particularly critical sanitary crisis.

As pointed out in the analysis of Campione et al. [10] the social, economical and technological environment of Mozambique poses some strict constraints to realize such analysis that in developed countries are normal Business Intelligence activities [2]. In particular [10] identifies the following challenges:

- lack of IT skills: qualified personnel, able to operate IT devices and tools is scarce and consequently the data collected is not trustworthy;
- lack of data: the diagnostic capability of the lower level point of care is rather poor compared to more specialized level of care (hospitals of level III or below have less diagnostic facilities than hospitals of level IV);
- territory highly distributed and sparsely populate: in order to get a comprehensive picture of the health state of population it is necessary to have a good coverage of the territory at the national level;
- infrastructure limitations: no electricity, no information communication technologies, no connectivity and no computers available;
- lack of information systems: there are neither the applications to manage health records nor the personal information of patients and consequently it is difficult to

identify patients in the long term and to maintain detailed information on their health story.

Data is typically collected on paper with significant manual effort and difficulties of communication and analysis by other parties at higher level of the hierarchy where planning and resource management is performed. The lack of computerization in the point of care, especially at the periphery, makes the data collection particularly difficult; with a considerable amount of time and manual effort required from the personnel. Furthermore, people are not motivated to spend effort in such a boring task as they do not see any useful results in short time coming out. These factors leave the data collection process incomplete and error-prone.

Indeed a great step forward has been performed with the adoption of a standardized list of diagnosis selected from the ICD-10 standard [4]. However, an IT solution capable of effectively supporting the collection of data, and is easy to install in critical environment with lack of infrastructure and is simple to use even for poorly trained people; is still missing. This solution should be general enough to be usable at any level of the national health care system with a great degree of flexibility and customizability to collect as much information as possible.

In this work we present the solution we provide in the context of the project "SIS-H – Módulo Internamentos" launched with internal tender by the Mozambican Ministry of Health (MISAU) according to the Mozambique eGovernment Strategy.

The main project goal is to rapidly overcome the lack of statistical information for hospitals of level III and level IV, devising software applications to collect and aggregate data in the clinical area, with specific focus on admissions and discharges of patients. Those aggregated data concern Maputo Central Hospital, Beira Central Hospital and Pemba Provincial Hospital and are being periodically sent to Provincial Health Offices and to the Ministry of Health, enabling analysis and planning on the health care system.

We provide a platform that effectively answers the challenges identified above both technical (lack of IT infrastructure) and organizational (data sources distributed on the territory with a hierarchical organization, few qualified human resources)[1].

We believe that a typical solution to perform business intelligence analysis realized for use in developed countries cannot be applied as-is in developing countries because the problems, the needs and the constraints are completely different. For that reason, we choose to work in strict collaboration with local companies and governmental organizations to bring our experience in the development of similar solutions in such critical context: which only domain experts living directly in contact with these problems could help us to fully understand.

2 Related Work

Mature technologies and methodologies are available in literature [2][13] for the design and development of data warehouse (DWH) systems that may serve our data

---

[1] Our solution brings new opportunities for the use of the same platform also in other domains, such as economy and education.

analysis problem. However, these approaches make some assumptions that are not valid in our context. First of all, they assume data can be extracted from IT systems at the data sources and centralized in a data warehouse. The problem is that in our case such IT systems are not always available (as in most of the cases they are not even present) and there is not (yet) a central data collector that could host a DWH.

Furthermore, classical DWH approaches assume an enterprise is highly motivated to create and maintain active a DWH sending timely information. In our case people acting as data collectors may be: not only employees of an organization but also volunteers, that should be motivated to collect timely and correct information; even if they do not understand or see immediately the positive effect of their work.

Another limitation is that these solutions typically assume a DWH is loaded basically in a real time mode, but in our case data may arrive with delays of weeks or not arrive at all.

Solutions for Business Intelligence available in the open source community like SpagoBI[2] or Talend[3] are interesting but too complex for our case as they provide many functionalities that in these contexts are not useful, and they risk to transform the solution into an unmanageable tool that nobody is able to use. Instead, we need to aim at simplicity with few and intuitive functionalities. Furthermore, these systems are general purpose BI applications that cannot be easily customized and cannot be adapted easily to different contexts. Besides, they require an amount of resources that in our case are not available; such as memory occupancy, local database and trained people to configure and customize the Extract, Transform and Load (ETL) [14] and reporting phases.

Developing an information integration solution using poor data quality is totally useless and also risky as it may lead to wrong results from the analysis and consequently wrong decisions. Conscious of this problem, we are currently studying approaches to trace and improve data quality and in particular to: keep the consumers of BI analysis (BI consumers) informed on the quality of the results they are using; trace and identify the sources and causes of mistakes with the help of the BI consumers by colleting suggestions on how to correct the mistakes; minimize the occurrence of the mistakes with tools to support critical phases of the data lifecycle, like data entry which is a task essentially with manual effort which is the primary cause of inconsistent data.

In this regard, we will pay a particular attention to the data entry and the cleaning phases and to the solutions already proposed in the research arena in the hope to reuse and extend them. For example, in [11] is proposed Usher, an end-to-end system to design forms that dynamically adapt to reduce the probability of errors during data entry (e.g. providing feedback in real-time to guide the data enterer toward more likely values).

The work in [1] extends the traditional Functional Dependencies into *Conditional functional dependencies* (CFDs) to capture the notion of "correct data" and to improve Data Cleaning tools in the detection and correction of inconsistencies and errors in the data.

---

[2] http://www.spagoworld.org/xwiki/bin/view/SpagoBI/
[3] http://www.talend.com/

As pointed out in [3] dirty data[4] often violates some integrity constraints reflecting organization's policies related to the quality of the data. To deal with this, [3] presents an approach that suggests possible rules and identifies conformant or non-conformant records (context-dependent rules).

3 Solution

Currently, healthcare services are monitored by collecting (often manually) data on the clinical process and sending hardcopy reports to districts, provinces and finally to the healthcare office (MISAU). Owing to some lacks on IT-systems and connections, data capture and analysis operations cannot always guarantee reliable and coherent information.

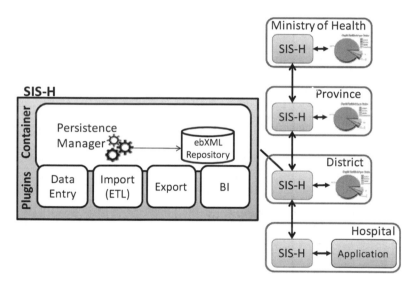

Fig. 1. Deployment of the SIS-H module in the healthcare hierarchical organization of Mozambique

We provide a generic communication infrastructure, SIS-H, to exchange data amongst facilities, across the whole healthcare system hierarchy – from operational units, hospitals, districts, provinces and up to the ministry – regardless of the available communication media (e.g., compact disk, usb stick, web-internet).

The SIS-H module could be replicated at the different sites of the Mozambique Healthcare organization and be applied also in other domains (e.g. to support the Ministry of Education and of the Interior). The caption in (Fig. 1) shows the main components of the module divided into a container managing data persistence (ebXML Repository) and a series of plugins providing the applicative functionalities and in particular: Data Entry, to support users to type in the system aggregated

---

[4] Not suitable for data analysis, with data problems such as inconsistency and incompleteness.

statistics on patient admissions and discharges that are collected on paper forms; Import (ETL), to load statistic data collected from other sites, typically from other levels of the organization; Export, to prepare an export of statistical information to be imported and used in another site, typically at a higher level of the hierarchy; BI, a module to produce business intelligence reports.

The next section presents a more detailed description of how the architecture works and in particular how the SIS-H module can produce an export that is understandable to installations in other sites allowing their interoperability.

3.1 Architecture

Each SIS-H plugin serves a dedicated purpose independently from the rest of the components so that modules can be changed or replaced without any impact on the rest of the system. This ensures greater flexibility, scalability and maintainability of the system. The main components of the architecture are the container and the various plugins for data Entry, data import (ETL), data export, and BI purposes.

The core functionalities of the system are given by the container which encapsulates a persistence manager (see Fig. 1). The Container is decomposed into five pillar features namely: *Plugin Manager*, *Workflow Manager*, *Data mapping/conversion Manager* and *Plugin Installation Manager*.

The *Plugin Manager* is responsible for associating user actions to dedicated plugins as well as loading configurations of the selected plugin. The *Workflow Manager* executes the workflow of the plugin by calling exposed methods through java reflection. The *Data mapping/conversion* manager transforms plugin internal data objects into the ebXML format (defined in [8]). Finally, the Plugin installation manager deals with addition and removal of plugins into the system. The behaviour of a plugin in terms of functionalities accessible by a certain user, data accessible and output formats are configured in the Plugin installation manager and can be easily updated to adapt to different contexts.

The SIS-H modules could be deployed in three flavours: centralized, client-server and embedded. In the *centralized* configuration, the basic layer contains the ebXML repository for data persistency while in the *distributed* case the ebXML repository is hosted in a remote application server as in Fig. 2. Finally, the *embedded* configuration is released with an embedded database (like Apache Derby[5]) for a fully portable system. The system can work both in a loosely connected environment and in a fully networked area[6].

It is worth mentioning that the application can support different languages and geographic regions through the use of ResourceBundle [12] residing outside the architecture, thus new languages can be added without changing the overall architecture of the system.

---

[5] http://db.apache.org/derby/

[6] On one hand, in remote areas where the network connectivity may be poor or even not be present, a fat client approach in which the application and persistency layer reside on the local machine or are embedded in the application would be suitable. On the other hand, in larger cities such as Maputo (the capital of Mozambique), equipped with network connectivity, the system can run in a client-server mode with LAN or internet configuration.

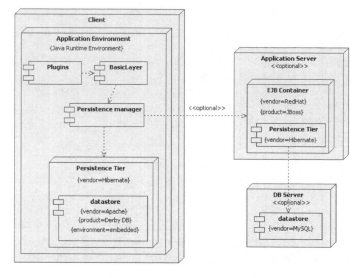

Fig. 2. Deployment diagram of the SIS-H application

3.2 Conceptual Model

Fig. 3 shows the organizational model of the hierarchical structure of the Mozambican health system. The healthcare facilities are organized in Health Care Units (health centers and clinics) and hospitals of different kinds (Specialized Hospital, Rural Hospital and so on). Each hospital is divided into departments which offer specific services. Each healthcare facility refers to an entity of the Government (e.g. the Province or MISAU) to which it must submit reports (known as *"ficha"*) on the activities performed. The data structure of such reports reflects at a conceptual level the internal operating procedures of hospitals and it is mapped internally and transferred from one level of the organizational hierarchy to the next in XML according to the ebXML standard.

Since there is no centralized database in which all the data is stored, it is vital not only to identify each *ficha* uniquely across different health units all the way up to the government administrative domain, but also to capture the organizational structure and the hierarchical level from which the *ficha* originates. In essence, each SIS-H module is aware of its location in the hierarchy of the health system. In this way it is simple to map other hierarchical organizations (for example, to add another hierarchical level, like an internal department or another top level administrative body like another ministry).

The adopted encoding for uniquely indentifying the *ficha* follows the hierarchy of the structure up to the service point in which the data was transferred. For example, if the operator that performs data export is registered in Maputo under Medicine department in section Surgery the unique identity of the *ficha* transferred would be as shown by the path element in Fig. 4.

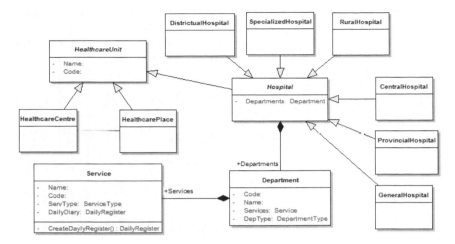

Fig. 3. Health system organizational model and relationships between units and structures of government

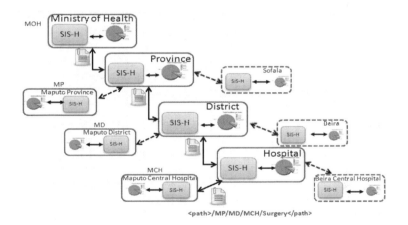

Fig. 4. *Ficha* flow and embedded organizational structure unique identity

4 Deployed Prototype

All the system is designed and developed according to open source principles and technologies. Fig. 5 shows the main form of the application to access to the following features: the Data Entry plugin, used for the daily registration of admissions and discharges of patients; the Export Plugin used to export the "*fichas*" XML files to exchange data; the Import Plugin to import the data previously exported by a different location; the BI Plugin, used to produce BI reports, in which we adopted Jasper Intelligence[7] as BI tool; and System Management used to manage the users, the general system configuration, backup procedures, etc.

---

[7] http://www.jaspersoft.com/

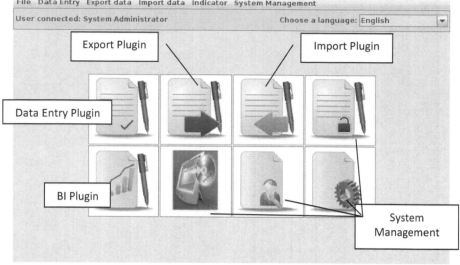

Fig. 5. Main Form sample, and the access to the Plugins

5   Conclusion and Future Work

Our modular architecture divided into plugin modules allows composing a suite of functionalities on the base of the needs and characteristic of the installation site. Plugins can be easily updated and configured to customize their behaviour and functionalities, data accessible and output formats to adapt to different contexts. The modular architecture allows for simple integration of specific functions based on flow type, control functions and validation information.

In the future, our architecture could be extended to manage other protocols and media, enabling the architecture to be applied in other contexts like the ministries of finance and education. Other extensions could introduce the research results on the quality of the data managed inside our architecture.

Acknowledgments. The project is headed by the Mozambican Ministry of Health (MISAU), collaborating with the Department for Information and Health (DIS), MOASIS (closely related with the University E. Mondlane) and the Consortium Pandora Box Ltda – GPI Spa. Our special thanks to Dra. Célia Gonçalves, Dr. Amisse Momade, all team at MISAU,   Dr. Alessandro Campione and all MOASIS team.

References

1. Bohannon, P., Fan, W., Geerts, F., Jia, X., Kementsietsidis, A.: Conditional functional dependencies for data cleaning. In: Proc. ICDE (2007)
2. The Data Warehouse Toolkit: The Complete Guide to Dimensional Modeling, 2nd edn. John Wiley & Sons, Chichester (2002)

3. Chiang, F., Miller, R.J.: Discovering data quality rules. Proceedings of the VLDB Endowment (2008)
4. World Health Organization. ICD-10: International Statistical Classification of Diseases and Related, Health Problems. 10th Revision,
   http://www.apps.who.int/classifications/apps/icd/icd10online/
5. World Health Organization. Mozambique, Mozambique's health system: Health and development, http://www.who.int/countries/moz/areas/health_system/en/index1.html
6. Ministério da Saúde, Plano Estratégico do sector Saúde, República de Moçambique (2007-2012), http://www.who.int/countries/moz/publications/pess_2007_2012.pdf
7. Ministry of health. Report on the revision of the data from HIV epidemiological surveillance. Round 2007. Republic of Mozambique (February 2008), http://www.misau.gov.mz/pt/content/download/4637/28101/file/Ronda2007EN.pdf
8. Standard ebXML: Registry Information Model, http://www.ebxml.org/specs/index.htm#technical_specifications
9. World Health Organization. Terms of Reference for Designing the Requirements of the Health Information System of the Maputo Central Hospital and preparation of the Tender Specifications. Technical Report. Version 2.0. (January 2007)
10. Pastore, R., Campione, A., Gonçalves, B., Melo, A., Goncalves, C., Matos, C.S., Mugai, M.: Use of ICD-10 for morbidity and mortality notification for in-patients, in recourse limited settings. The experience of Mozambique using reduced disease lists. Annual meeting of the WHO Family of International Classifications Network
11. Chen, K., Chen, H., Conway, N., Hellerstein, J.: Usher: Improving data quality with dynamic forms. In: ICDE (2010)
12. Sun Microsystems. Java Resource Bundle, http://java.sun.com/j2se/1.4.2/docs/api/java/util/ResourceBundle.html
13. Chaudhuri, S., Dayal, U.: An overview of data warehousing and OLAP technology. ACM Sigmod Record (1997)
14. Kimball, R., Caserta, J.: The Data Warehouse ETL Toolkit: Practical Techniques for Extracting, Cleaning, Conforming, and Delivering Data. John Wiley & Sons, Chichester (2004)

Emerginov: How Free Software Can Boost Local Innovation, a Win-Win Deal between Operator and Local Innovation Partners

Morgan Richomme, Geerish Suddul, Rai Basgeet, and Avinash Soobul

AFRICOMM 2010

2nd International ICST Conference on e-Infrastructure and e-Services for Developing Countries
25-26 November 2010 – Cape Town, South Africa
morgan.richomme@orange-ftgroup.com, g.suddul@utm.intnet.mu,
{rai.basgeet,avinash.soobul}@mauritiustelecom.com

Abstract. This paper deals with the description of a new co-innovation method linking an operator and academic resources. This method based on the promotion of free software has been validated during Orange Expo 2010 Mauritius organized by Mauritius Telecom. The goal is to boost local innovation and ease the development of "Telcoweb" micro-services.

Keywords: Co-innovation, free software, micro-service, SMS, Voice.

1 Introduction

Lots of telecommunication services do not meet expectations on emerging markets. Most of them, usually designed for countries where network constraints are low, consists in flavoring standard American or European services. Such services are thus complex, do not correspond neither to the need of local people nor to the local usage.

However micro-services, bridging Telecommunication world (GSM is widely available in emerging countries) and web worlds (expertise and collective intelligence in the network), could have a real impact on development [1] by providing ad-hoc services for people developed by local innovation partners connected to the reality of the field. Several studies showed how SMS based service [4] could have an impact on development.

Co-innovating with local partners is indeed a good way to change this paradigm. However such co-innovation requires several conditions; local resources to develop services, a shared, open and low-cost infrastructure and finally a connexion to the telecommunication network.

Mauritius Telecom, in partnership with Orange Labs initiated such initiative with 2 universities of Mauritius. This paper will detail the infrastructure, the co-innovation process as well as the results of a first set of services developed by the academic resources within 1 month.

R. Popescu-Zeletin et al. (Eds.): AFRICOMM 2010, LNICST 64, pp. 132–140, 2011.
© Institute for Computer Sciences, Social Informatics and Telecommunications Engineering 2011

2   A Low-Cost IP Infrastructure

The goal of the infrastructure is to provide a bridge between GSM and IP worlds. Additionally the architecture shall be open, shared and duplicable. It may be compared to Intelligent Network because it provides added value services on top of the GSM network using the richness and flexibility of IP. Several initiatives from NGO or universities already contributed to selected FLOSS[1] (Free/Libre/Open Source software) components to build open web platforms mainly for e-learning [2] or health services.

2.1   Architecture

The architecture can be displayed as follow:

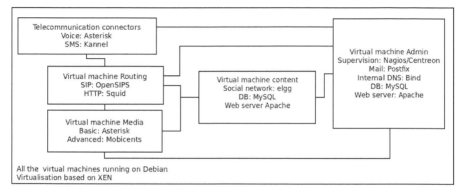

Fig. 1. Emerginov architecture

We distinguish 5 main parts

- **Telecommunication** functions: these functions consist in all the gateways between traditional telecommunication infrastructure (SMSC, switch) and the IP platform.
- **Routing** functions: the platform supports two signaling protocols, SIP for VoIP telecommunication and HTTP(S) for web
- **Media** functions: these functions may include the management of vocal announcements, voice mail, conference bridge, voice recognition
- **Content** function: these functions include social network, a multimedia library usable by all the developers, promoting content under creative common license or in public domain.
- **Administration** functions: mainly supervision

The telecommunication functions require dedicated hardware. All the other IP functions are virtualized to save power supply and optimize the machine usage.

---

[1] http://en.wikipedia.org/wiki/Free_and_open_source_software

2.2 Promoting Free Software

Free software was the only way to achieve our goals [10] for two main reasons: the design and the adoption of the platform.

The design shall be cost-effective. It shall also integrate the possibility of a local support. Free softwares selected on the platform can all be considered as mature. Local expertise already exists and academic resources, that can be considered as future support, have also a high knowledge of the selected components.

Free software was also imperative to facilitate the adoption of the components then to simplify the developments themselves. In fact any student was able to download any of the components and could thus start developing in a local environment before pushing his/her code to the platform.

The main different components can be described in the following table.

Table 1. Main Free softwares integrated in the innovation platform

Component	Role	Comments
Debian/Xen	OS and virtualization layer	http://www.debian.org/ http://www.xen.org/
OpenSIPS	SIP router (telco part)	http://www.opensips.org/
Squid	HTTP router	http://www.squid-cache.org/
Asterisk	IP/PSTN gateway, Interactive Voice Response and Conference bridge	Asterisk is the media toolbox of the platform. Associated with tools such as audacity, sox, it provides a complete set of media applications http://www.asterisk.org/
Kannel	SMS/WAP gateway	http://www.kannel.org/
LAMP	Linux, Apache, MySQL, PHP	http://www.apache.org/ http://dev.mysql.com/
Elgg	Social network for developers	provides the links towards the forums but aims to ease the exchange of best practice regarding micro services. http://elgg.org/

Free software is an opportunity for the operator to provide innovation in emerging countries. In developed countries, the adoption of free software for telecommunication is not so easy because it modifies the traditional privileged relations between an operator and its suppliers. Support and maintenance of free softwares shall be managed through third party companies not always familiar with operator context. In Emerging countries the choice is sometimes: "free software or nothing". It requires then to internalize some risks.

2.3 Towards an Innovation Consortium

Assuming that a platform is connected to the networks (IP and telecom), the key challenge is to build a complete ecosystem with partners of innovation [3]. All the actors shall see their interest to co-innovate. An innovation consortium shall be designed detailing the rights and the obligations of each of the members.

Table 2. Innovation consortium: main roles

	Rights	**Obligations**
Operator	Provide marketing support	Provide and operate the platform
	Provide technical support	Provide legal support
	Suspend telecommunication resources	Provide telecommunication resources
	(phone or SMS numbers), in case of	Do not put any micro service to
	misuse of these resources	production before agreement with the
		innovation partner
		Do not copy or recode a microservice
		without innovation partner agreement
Innovation	Design of the micro applications	Respect free software licenses
partner	Keep the paternity of the source code	Provide source code under free license
		Discuss with associated operator first
		when moving to production

The goal is to build a shared library of business applications for emerging countries. Any innovation partner joining the consortium could capitalize on previous projects. Thus free software would not be located only into middleware but also in applicative layers. Adullact, OSOR[2] are already referencing free software business applications (400 applications on health, education, associations, administration in adullact).

3   A "Telcoweb" Development Framework to Boost Co-innovation

3.1   Co-innovating

Emerginov is a platform but not a service. Services shall come from the innovation partners. The platform can be considered as the "engineering of the innovation" .

For academic resources there are two ways for co-innovation: develop micro-services or upgrade the platform.

3.2   Developing Micro-services

The development toolkit on top of the platform relies without surprise on open standards. A micro services will deal with a very limited number of lines of code. Each service will integrate existing components and web open API. Most of the micro services will deal with LAMP (web part), Asterisk extensions (vocal part), java/C/C++ and script languages.

The telco part managed through Asterisk or Kannel gateways, will be almost transparently managed by the operator. Concrete examples of micro services will be provided in next chapter.

3.3   Upgrading the Platform

Improving the platform to provide new useful features adapted to emerging countries is an important axis of co-innovation. This upgrade can consist in adding new components or update existing components according to local context.

---

[2] http://www.adullact.org/, http://forge.osor.eu

For example, it is interesting to add features dealing with local languages. In fact literacy rate is low on the region, and, in the same time, lots of languages coexist. Vocal recognition or Text To Speech functions do not exist in vernacular languages. The diversity of languages prevent any industrial from delivering such tools at a reasonable price. The operator can thus finance academic resources to work on existing FLOSS components (in this example Julius[3]) in order to adapt it to the local context.

3.4 Towards a Digital Free Software Patrimony

A mentioned below, the ultimate goal of Emerginov is to create an autonomous ecosystem where the operator and the partners of the innovation will contribute to create a shared digital patrimony with tools and content . All services will obviously not survive following the traditional Darwinian life cycle of FLOSS components. Anyway a library of micro services will be ready to be re-used and the best services could be quickly deployable in any emerging countries.

4 Field Experimentation: Orange Expo 2010

4.1 Codecamp

The Emerginov concept relied on the basic principle of free software and hence the main idea was to provide open APIs for developers and academic institutions to gain access to the so long well secured Telco platforms. The objectives were to:

- facilitate the merging of Web and mobile users.
- encourage the development of web related services using Telco architecture as base.
- use Orange as a common platform for different academic institutions and promote academic knowledge sharing.
- develop long term relationship between academic institutions an Orange as operator.

Mauritius Telecom (MT) hence initiated actions to bring the Emerginov concept into the life of Mauritians Academia.   Resources were assigned to the project as MT planned to use the Orange Expo 2010 exhibition to boost the introduction of Emerginov. It was hence an ideal platform for the demonstration of the concrete collaboration of telecommunication industry with academia to produce product and services that were wholly developed by local people to address the local market needs.

The figure below illustrates the process that were put in place to achieve the objective of MT and Orange Lab and eventually the objectives of the academia.

A stand was hence dedicated to the Emerginov concept at Orange Expo as it was going to be one of the highlight of the show, and indeed was very positively appraised

---

[3] http://julius.sourceforge.jp/en_index.php

by the visitors. Students from the University of Mauritius (UOM) and the University of Technology (UTM) demonstrated six locally developed applications   which attracted over 10,000 visitors to the stand.   The best projects were chosen through and on-line voting system (GSM and Web) itself hosted on the Emerginov platform.

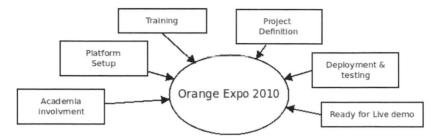

Fig. 2. Innovation process

Besides the possibility to work on research products and services using platforms based on free software, MT wants to move further ahead by providing students the opportunity to develop applications which can be used in the real world or even be marketed abroad.

Through this initiative, Mauritius Telecom wants to establish a bridge with local academic institutions and to get the opportunity to reveal hidden potentials of students and promote local developers and entrepreneurship in the ICT sector.

Table 3. List of micro applications

Name	Description	DevTime (Man-days)	Number Lines of Code
Traffic Watch (UTM)	Traffic Information on highway in Mauritius. Available on micro-browsers and full blown web browsers.	20	750
Buddy Locator (UTM)	A friend finder using GPS enabled mobile phones.	15	1000
SmsNot (UTM)	A developer SMS Notification API which helps to build web and mobile based Short Message System Applications.	15	2000
Shopping Buddy (UoM)	SMS based application providing information on shops ranked through a Facebook application. An additional administration page allows shops to provide vouchers.	15	< 2000
Call To Play (UoM)	Transform GSM hanset into a gamepad for remote control of a game through DTMF	15	< 500

4.2 List of Micro-services

Six projects that have commercial potential and usefulness in the local market have been produced within less than 1 month. the projects were mainly SMS and Web based and some even used the GPS localization API provided by Google Maps. The projects in fact followed the market trend , where we have over 2.5 millions SMS sent daily and over 1 millions mobile users and over 70 ,000 broadband connections in a population of 1.2 million people.

4.3 Focus on Traffic Watch

One of the most appreciated service developed over the platform by UTM is entitled Traffic Watch. The main aim behind this micro service was to provide information on the evolution of traffic over the highways in Mauritius. The core idea was to make traffic information available in near real-time anytime and anywhere, over mobile devices and demonstrate the prototype during the Orange Expo 2010.

4.3.1 Objectives behind Traffic Watch
One persistent problem in Mauritius is traffic jam during peak hours, especially on the main highways (M1 and M2). Currently in the local context, traffic information is only available to the public from local FM radio stations but the limitation is that, these details are aired at a specific time. If someone happens to miss the traffic news, then the latter is completely in the dark about traffic situation. All these traffic information is actually being collected by the Mauritius Police Force, and kept in a non IS based system at their central division. Another point which we noted is that traffic density changes radically in a small lapse of time. Thus, traffic news which was valid a moment ago might no longer be relevant after a few minutes.

In Mauritius according to recent statistics [7], the Mobidensity in Mauritius (mobile phones per 100 inhabitants) is now 84.3% and still rising. We segmented these 84.3% mobile subscribers, for the year 2009 and noticed that mobile internet subscribers attained 52.5%. Again, from [7] the population covered by mobile cellular telephony is defined as the number of inhabitants who live within areas covered by a mobile cellular network, irrespective of whether or not they subscribe to the service. Since 2009, 99.0% of the population is covered by mobile cellular telephony.

Based on the above description and statistics, it can be deduced that implementing a system as the Traffic Watch in our local mobile market would nearly reach the whole population. For the mobile operator, this would represent an interesting potential in terms of revenue.

4.3.2 Architecture of Traffic Watch
In an attempt to keep traffic information accessible, we devised an architecture which keeps all information in a generic format (XML). As mentioned before, availability of traffic information is one objective of the system. The architecture thus allows users to access traffic information in the following ways:

- On a micro-browser (web enabled mobile phone) which supports javascript (Safari and Opera). This is the ideal way to view traffic information with a map and different icons representing the three different states.
- A plain GSM enabled phone. Traffic information is pushed by SMS to all subscribed users.
- On a full blown Web browser. For web and special users like the content provider (Mauritius Police Force).

The system takes the form a Web application with a series of other components which are illustrated in Figure below.

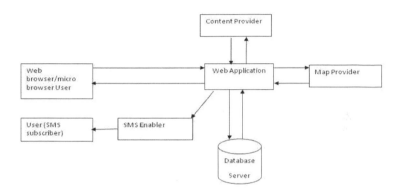

Fig. 3. Traffic watch architecture

Web Application. In the attempt to provide a fully inter-operable system, a web application has been devised, which is at the heart of the architecture above. PHP has been used as server side programming language, with AJAX techniques to request map data. The database is MySQL and is used for persistent storage.

Map Provider. The ideal application will display a map on the mobile phone web browser, which allows better interaction with the users. This is the only component which is not part of the Emerginov platform. Google Map API was chosen in this case since it has proven to be fully compatible with components on Emerginov.

SMS Enabler. The application is not only targeted towards 3G mobile phones but 2.5G and 2G as well. The SMS enabler component plays this role. It consists of the SmsNot API also developed by UTM, Kannel SMS gateway, and the operator's SMSC.

Content Provider Interface. The content provider is the Mauritius Police Force. Multiple traffic agents at the main round-abouts and junctions during peak hours, collect traffic information, which are centralized at their main operation room. This same information can be fed into the system via a specialized interface to the web application. This interface is secured with an encrypted password.

4.3.3 Flexibility of the Architecture

Any application with an XML parser would be able to read the traffic messages and do further processing if required. The architecture has been implemented in a layered approach, which allows easy integration and debugging. We have done integration with the Asterisk server, whereby policemen can record a status of the traffic that is automatically broadcasted on a web radio.

4.3.4 Limitations of Traffic Watch and Future Work

OpenStreetMap [9] could be seen as an alternative to Google MAP API as it is based on a full free software solution (unlike google). A vocal kiosk or an USSD connector could be studied.

5 Conclusions

Building a local innovation ecosystem is a key challenge for development in emerging countries. An operator is a key actor of micro-services based on mobile. Telecommunication companies are usually very present on the field unlike international web actors. Therefore an operator can bridge the two worlds, connecting end users to the richness of IP worlds. To achieve the stimulation of the eco-system, the operator shall provide an infrastructure, support and associate local actors. That is the goal of the Emerginov consortium.

References

1. Duflo, E.: Le développement humain, Lutter contre la pauvreté (I). Seuil (2010)
2. Tsietsi, M., Shibeshi, Z., Terzoli, A., Wells, G.: An Asterisk-based framework for E-learning using open protocols and open source software. Rhodes University, Department of Computer Science, Grahamstown, South Africa (2009)
3. Wu, S., Jin, J., Chen, J., Vanhaverbeke, W.: Open innovation strategy in the process of technological capability development: Conceptual framework aspect. In: 16th International Conference on Industrial Engineering and Engineering Management, IE&EM 2009, Digital Object identifier (2009)
4. Houssian, A., Kilany, M., Korenblum, J.: Mobile phone job services: Linking developing-country youth with employers, via SMS. In: International Conference on Information and Communication Technologies and Development (ICTD), Digital Object Identifier (2009)
5. Davaa, T.: Free and Open Source Software development in Mongolia. Mongolian University of Science and Technology, Ulaanbaatar (2007)
6. Collins, L.: Cutting the cost of computing. Engineering & Technology (2007)
7. National Computer Board, Information Society Outlook. ICT Indicator Newsletter 1(1) (April 2010)
8. Google Maps/Google Earth APIs Terms of Service, http://code.google.com/apis/maps/terms.html
9. Open Street Map API, http://wiki.openstreetmap.org/wiki/API
10. ran Reijswoud, V., Toppi, C.: Alternative routes in the digital world, Open Source Software in Africa, http://opensource.mit.edu/papers/reijswoudtopi.pdf

Author Index

Printed by Publishers' Graphics LLC
BT20130311.19.21.54